D.F.M. STRAUSS

THE PHILOSOPHY OF HERMAN DOOYEWEERD

PAIDEIA
PRESS

www.paideiapress.ca
www.reformationaldl.org

The Philosophy of Herman Dooyeweerd

A publication of Paideia Press (3248 Twenty First St., Jordan Station, Ontario, Canada L0R 1S0).

© 2021 by Paideia Press. All rights reserved.

All rights reserved. Except for brief quotations in critical publications or reviews, no part of this book may be reproduced in any manner without prior written permission from Paideia Press at the address above.

Cover Art and Book Design by Steven R. Martins

ISBN 978-0-88815-280-0

Printed in the United States of America

CONTENTS

WESTERN PHILOSOPHY	7
ULTIMATE COMMITMENTS	11
THEORETICAL AND SUPRA-THEORETICAL ASSUMPTIONS	13
GROUND MOTIVES	17
THE GREEK GROUND-MOTIVE OF MATTER AND FORM	18
THE BIBLICAL GROUND MOTIVE	21
THE SCHOLASTIC MOTIVE OF NATURE AND GRACE	23
THE HUMANISTIC GROUND-MOTIVE OF NATURE AND FREEDOM	26
DOOYEWEERD AND KANT	31
POST-KANTIAN PHILOSOPHY	36
THE BASIC CONTOURS OF DOOYEWEERD'S PHILOSOPHY	39
THE THEORY OF MODAL LAW-SPHERES	39
SUBJECT FUNCTIONS AND OBJECT FUNCTIONS	40
THE MULTI-ASPECTUAL NATURE OF HUMAN BEINGS	42
RETROCIPATIONS AND ANTICIPATIONS ON THE LAW SIDE AND FACTUAL SIDE	43

PRIMITIVE TERMS	48
THE ELEMENTARY BASIC CONCEPTS OF THE ACADEMIC DISCIPLINES	51
THE COMPOUND BASIC CONCEPTS OF THE ACADEMIC DISCIPLINES	53
DISCLOSURE AS A DEEPENING OF MEANING	60
CONTRADICTION AND ANTINOMY	66

THE DIMENSION OF ONTIC TIME — 71

DO WE LIVE IN A "SPACE-TIME CONTINUUM"?	74
TIME AND THE IMPASSE OF POSITIVISM	75

THE DIMENSION OF (NATURAL AND SOCIETAL) ENTITIES — 87

UNDIFFERENTIATED SOCIETIES	93
THE STATE WITHIN A DIFFERENTIATED SOCIETY	97

THE LEGACY OF REFORMATIONAL PHILOSOPHY — 107

SELECTED LIST OF SOURCES — 111

INDICES — 129

NAME INDEX	131
SUBJECT INDEX	139

ABOUT THE AUTHOR — 144

HERMAN DOOYEWEERD (1894-1977) was born in Amsterdam. He established the *Philosophy of the Cosmonomic Idea* (a philosophy which explicitly gives an account of the laws holding for the cosmos) and taught the *Encyclopedia of the Science of Law* (philosophy of law) from 1926 until 1964 at the *Free University* of Amsterdam.

1912-1917: University: Studying at the Free University of Amsterdam.

1917: Ph.D. dissertation, completed: De Ministerraad in het Nederlandsche Staatsrecht [The Cabinet in Dutch Constitutional Law].

1918: Work in tax office, Haarlingen, Friesland.

1918: Legal advisor for municipal government in Leiden.

1919-22: Post at Health Office, Dept. of Labour, The Hague, examining draft legislation.

1922 approx: His idea of law-spheres (modal aspects) originates.

1922-26: Work at the Kuyper Institute, The Hague; a time of intense study and writing, during which the idea of law-spheres received its first theoretical articulation.

1926: Appointed as professor in the Faculty of Law at the *Vrije Universiteit* (Free University), Amsterdam (retire in 1964).

The explanation below intends to highlight briefly some of the key distinctions and insights of Dooyeweerd's philosophy. In some respects it will be done with reference to states of affairs also recognized by scholars who are working with a theoretical frame of reference different than the approach found in Dooyeweerd's philosophy. He never wanted to exclude any intellectual tradition from the "denkgemeenschap" (*thought-community*) of the West. Therefore this overview of his philosophy aims at stepping into his shoes while at the same time expounding his systematic insights in confrontation with diverse philosophical and special scientific orientations.

Western Philosophy

WESTERN PHILOSOPHY originated in Greek antiquity and was transformed during the medieval period attempting to obtain a synthesis between Greek philosophy and biblical Christianity. It eventually continued its path via the Renaissance and Enlightenment up to our present day. During the past 500 years it was largely dominated by diverse humanistic intellectual traditions.

The first radical Christian philosophical movement that developed systematic philosophical insights while taking distance from un-biblical motives present in the thought of major thinkers such as Augustine (354-430) and Thomas Aquinas (1225-1277), emerged in a tradition dating back to the Reformation of the sixteenth century and eventually was continued by Groen van Prinsterer (1801-1876) and Abraham Kuyper (1837-1920). These thinkers in particular paved the way for the contribution of Herman Dooyeweerd (1894-1977) who, alongside with his brother-in-law D. H. Th Vollenhoven (1892-1978), developed a philosophical understanding of reality directed and informed by the biblical distinction between Creator and creation – an approach liberating philosophy from the antinomous impasse of reductionist *isms* (to which we shall return below).

Regarding the repute of Dooyeweerd's philosophy, as found in the assessment of various scholars (coming from different backgrounds), the following appreciative statements are significant:

> (i) "...the most original philosopher Holland has produced, even Spinoza not excepted" – Prof. G.E. Langemeijer (former Attorney General of the Dutch Appeal Court and a former Chairman of the Royal Dutch Academy of Sciences – he is not a Christian – 1965).

> (ii) "...the most profound, innovative, and penetrating philosopher since Kant" – Giorgio Delvecchio (a well-known Italian neo-Kantian philosopher).

> (iii) "Herman Dooyeweerd is undoubtedly the most formidable Dutch philosopher of the 20th century. ...As a humanist I have always looked at 'my own tradition' in search for similar examples. They simply don't exist" – Dr. P.B. Cliteur (President of the 'Humanist League' in The Netherlands and Professor of philosophy at the Technical University of Delft – 1994).

> (iv) An internationally well-known Dutch philosopher, C.A. Van Peursen (who was practically throughout his life-time a critical conversation-partner radically differing from Dooyeweerd and who influenced many philosophers worldwide), at the end of his life remarked that many

books written within the domain of philosophy of science should not have been written had the authors familiarized themselves with Dooyeweerd's insights (1995).

Ultimate Commitments

BY DISTINGUISHING between the motivating root-commitment of scholarly thinking and the theoretical distinctions involved in understanding the cohering diversity within creation, the *Philosophy of the Cosmonomic Idea* avoids metaphysical speculation, takes serious the states of affairs revealed by the various special sciences (the natural sciences and the humanities) and encourages scholarly communication across the boundaries of alternative (and even opposing) philosophical orientations.

Dooyeweerd uses the term "religion" in two different but related senses:

1. It may refer to the radical, central and integral depth dimension of creation, touching the *heart* or I-ness of the human being, giving direction to all the issues of life proceeding from this core dimension.

2. It may designate one amongst the many articulations of life, familiar to us in faith and confessional activities and found alongside other human endeavours differentiated in activities such as thinking, the forming of culture, lingual activities, social actions, economic con-

cerns, aesthetic creations, the formation of law, and moral worries.

In English, the word *religion* is normally used to designate only the *faith function* of reality and the activities qualified by it, namely the so-called "religious activities". The important distinction is therefore between religion in the aspectual sense of *faith* and *religion* in its life-encompassing *radical* and *integral* sense – where *radical* means *touching the root of* human *existence*, and *integral* means embracing *all of life*.

During the last part of the 19th century renewed reflection on the relation of the Christian religion, in its radical and integral sense, to science, culture, and society was done. It motivated Abraham Kuyper, under whose inspiring leadership this new reflection occurred, to point out that the great movement of the Reformation could not continue to be restricted to the reformation of church and theology. Its biblical point of departure touches on the religious root of the whole of temporal life and had to assert its validity in all of its sectors for, as an all-embracing world view, it is clearly distinguishable from both Roman Catholicism and Humanism.

~~~

In 1917 Herman Dooyeweerd completed his legal studies with a dissertation entitled: *De Ministerraad in het Nederlandsche staatsrecht* (*The Cabinet in Dutch Constitutional Law*). During the early 1920s he broadened his perspective by contemplating general philosophical problems, including an in-depth study of the history of philosophy and closely related to an extensive study investigating "[T]he Struggle for a Christian Politics." During this period he developed his new philosophical insights in close cooperation with his brother-in-law, D. Theodor H. Vollenhoven, who wrote a dissertation on the foundations of mathematics in 1918.

Theoretical and supra-theoretical assumptions

When Dooyeweerd was appointed at the Free University of Amsterdam in 1926 the development of a new philosophical orientation was reflected in a comprehensive *Inaugural Lecture* on the theme, *The Significance of the Cosmonomic Idea for the Science of Law and Legal Philosophy* (Free University, Amsterdam, October 15, 1926). A mere glimpse of the extensive footnotes of this address clearly indicates that it significantly exceeded the expectations of a normal Inaugural one. During the next decade he published a work on [*T*] *he Crisis in Humanistic Political Theory* (1931) followed by his magnum opus, *De Wijsbegeerte der Wetsidee* appeared in 1935-1936.

This was eventually updated and expanded in its English translation: *A New Critique of Theoretical Thought* (NC: 1953-1958 – 4 volumes). Besides numberless articles covering a wide range of academic disciplines ("special sciences"), Dooyeweerd's main academic work since his inaugural address focused on the science of law. This work comprises four Volumes and it represents an entirely new encyclopedic method of analyzing reality as well as formulating the basic concepts of the various academic disciplines. Dooyeweerd first wanted to see if his new philosophical understanding of reality proved to be fruitful for a special scientific discipline, such as the *science of law* (his own field of specialization), before he ventured to make public its general philosophical implications, as explained in *De Wijsbegeerte der Wetsidee* and *A New Critique of Theoretical Thought*.

Dooyeweerd addresses the *state of affairs* that although adherents of different philosophical schools of thought "profess" that their theories are purely theoretical, they nonetheless do not succeed in convincing each other. He calls this trust in human reason the *dogma* of the *autonomy of theoretical thought*. The aim of his transcendental critique of theoretical thought is to show that theoretical thought cannot find its starting point within itself, because then one or another aspect (mode of being) will be elevated to be the sole *mode of explanation* for all of reality – the source of the multiple *isms* found within philosophy and the various scholarly disciplines (such as physicalism, historicism, legalism, vitalism, arithmeticism, economism, and so on). Dooyeweerd contends that only when it is realized that the starting point of theoretical thought must transcend the diversity of aspects within creation, will it be possible to realize that it requires a supra-theoretical point of departure which is not only *radical* (touching the root of human existence) and *integral* (all-encompassing), but which is also in the grip of a *supra-theoretical religious ground-motive*. It is the religious ground-motive that ultimately directs theoretical thought through a provisional, fallible and improvable hypothesis of scholarly thinking, designated by Dooyeweerd as the *transcendental ground-idea* (theoretical view of reality).

What Dooyeweerd here advocates precedes significant insights emerging from the developments in the philosophy of science of the 20th century, namely acknowledging a theoretical frame of reference (a theoretical view of reality or *paradigm*), and realizing that human rationality is not self-sufficient. The long-standing trust in reason proceeded from a faith in reason which is not *rational* in itself. Twentieth century philosophers from different philosophical traditions started to acknowledge this fact. Karl Popper, for example, rejects what he calls an uncritical or comprehensive rationalism based upon "the principle that any assumption which cannot be supported either by argument or by experience is to be discarded." According to him this kind of rationalism is demonstrably inconsistent, i.e. in terms of its own criteria: since "all arguments must proceed from assumptions, it is plainly impossible to demand that all assumptions should be based on argument." Popper is also aware of the fact that behind the idea of an "assumptionless" approach, a huge *assumption* hides itself – something eventually also criticized by the prominent hermeneutical philosopher, Hans-Georg Gadamer (1989), who mocks the prejudice of Enlightenment against prejudices, while Dooyeweerd distinguishes between *theoretical prejudices* (the transcendental ground-idea) and *supra-theoretical prejudices* (the ground-motive). Popper knows that the rationalistic trust in reason is not rational itself, and explicitly speaks of "an irrational faith in reason" (1966-II) – which means that, according to him "rationalism is necessarily far from comprehensive or self-contained." Another formidable philosopher of science from the second half of the 20th century, Stegmüller (1969), holds a similar conviction when he says that there is no single domain in which a self-guarantee of human thinking exists – one already has to believe in something in order to justify something else.

What are these ground-motives?

Ground-Motives

AS TRUE COMMUNAL driving forces Dooyeweerd discerns *four* religious ground-motives operative within the history of Western civilization. He points out that three of them are *dialectical* since they are burdened by an inner dualism, which constantly induces them to spawn positions in which one pole is set irretrievably in diametrical opposition to the other. It is not only the development of theoretical thought that is ruled by these ground-motives, because the religious dynamics entailed in them lies at the foundation of Western cultural development as a whole.

Dooyeweerd identifies the following four ground-motives:

1. the form-matter motive of Greek antiquity;

2. the Scriptural ground-motive of creation, the fall into sin, and redemption through Christ Jesus in the communion of the Holy Spirit;

3. the Scholastic motive of religious synthesis, introduced by Roman Catholicism, that of nature and grace, which attempts to reconcile the former two motives;

4. the modern humanistic ground-motive of nature and freedom, in which the attempt is made to bring all of the earlier motives into an immanent (*diesseitige*) religious synthesis, concentrated in the human personality.

The Greek ground-motive of matter and form

Dooyeweerd distinguishes between the motive of *form*, *measure* and *harmony* on the one hand and the *matter* motive of the ever-flowing stream of life on the other. He explains the latter as follows:

> This was the motive of the divine, eternally flowing stream of life. Arising from mother earth, this stream of life periodically, in the cycle of time, brings forth everything that has individual form and shape; but then, inevitably, the latter falls prey to blind, unpredictable fate, to dread *Anankè* (necessity), in order that the eternally flowing and formless stream of life might continue on with its cycle of birth, death, and rebirth. This divine stream of life, coursing through everything that has bodily form, is a psychic fluid, which is not bound to the limits of the bodily form and thus cannot die with the latter, but which is conceived of nevertheless as material and earthly. The deepest mystery of the 'psyche' lies in an ecstatic transcending of one's bodily limits in a mystical absorption into the divine totality of life. In the words of Heraclitus, the obscure thinker of Ephesus, "You could not in your going find the ends of the soul... so deep is its law (logos)".

Dooyeweerd holds that both the matter motive and the form motive are ultimate in the sense of touching the heart as religious root or self-hood of being human. Since they are mutually exclusive and mutually dependent, the only option for a dialectical motive is to give *primacy* to one of its poles, without escaping from the opposite one. Initially, in Greek nature philosophy, the matter motive acquired the primacy in Greek thought.

The Ionian philosophers observed that amidst all *change* and *transition*, there must be something *persistent*. They proceeded from elements with a fluid divine nature (water, air, fire). Although Anaximander chose for the infinite-unlimited, the *apeiron*, his second and third Fragments asserted that the *apeiron* "is everlasting and ageless" and it "is immortal and indestructible." In a naturalistic shape the form motive clearly surfaced in the thought of Parmenides concerning the *unity* (oneness) of *being*. Empedocles subsequently distinguished four immutable *ontic forms* which he treated, as Aristotle notes, as if they were two: *fire* on the one hand and *earth*, *air* and *water* together on the other. The striking advance in the dialectical development of Greek philosophy noticeable here, is that Empedocles introduced two soul forces, love (*philia*) an animosity (*neikos*), where *philia* is a divine soul force and *neikos* is a non-divine soul force. This entails that the matter motive is only partially de-divinized – namely in connection with the *neikos*.

The decisive switch in assigning primacy to the form motive occurs in the thought of Anaxagoras. He elevated the *nous* (reason) to a self-existent state not limited or mixed with material sperms: "Other things all contain a part of everything, but Mind is infinite and self-ruling, and is mixed with no Thing, but is alone by itself ... For it [*nous*] is the finest of all Things, and the purest, and have complete understanding of everything, and has the greatest power (πάντον νοῦς κρατεῖ) (translation by Freeman). The *de-divinization* of the rigid, motionless and disorderly germs of matter clearly follows from the fact that now only the *nous* is designated as divine.

The atomists, Leucippus and Democritus, broke the indivisible static form of being of Parmenides up into a multiplicity of immutable stereometric forms, while they viewed matter as a void (*kenon*) which is unlimited and formless. In the thought of Socrates the divine *nous* of Anaxagoras continues as *form-giver* of the cosmos and as the origin of what is good and beautiful in the cosmos. Thus Socrates deepened the primacy of the form motive towards the concentration of all knowledge on the *good* and *beauty*. In the first Platonic dialogues this dynamic tendency plays a dominating role.

The dualism of matter and form in Plato's thought is foremost evident in his dualistic understanding of the intelligible world and the world of becoming. The ideal forms serve as *Urbilder* (archetypical forms) which are copied into transitory forms within which they are present. The split between the two principles of origin, form and (formless) matter, entails that within the world of becoming *copies* of the original ontic forms are found – each *eidos* has multiple *Abbilder* (copies). But Plato did realize that within the world of supra-sensory static forms there is no form for the formless (matter). Subsequent to his dialogue *Parmenides* Plato therefore contemplated an *ideal matter* (*eidetic matter*) (*hulè*), particularly in the *Timaeus*, in order to find an *original form* for matter amongst the other *eidè* (see the extensive discussion in Dooyeweerd 2003).

Against the background of Dooyeweerd's philosophy one can say that whereas Plato stumbled upon the law side of the cosmos as an *order for*, Aristotle transposed the transcendent ideas of Plato by equating them with the universal side (orderliness) of individual entities, conceived as the universal secondary substance which was supposed to unite form (actuality) and matter (potentiality). In his extensive work on the term *matter* in the philosophy of Aristotle we have to note how Happ discerns the mutuality and mutual exclusivity of the principles of matter and form. Moreover, it should be kept in mind that the biblical idea of creation is foreign to Greek philosophy. The latter accepted the slogan *ex nihilo nihil fit* (nothing comes from nothing).

The biblical ground-motive

The second ground-motive is that of creation, the fall into sin, and redemption through Christ Jesus in the communion of the Holy Spirit.

Tying in with Old Testament Judaism, the Christian religion introduced this theme into Western thought as a new communal religious motive, which, already in its doctrine of creation, placed itself in diametrical opposition to the ground-motive of ancient philosophy.

As the authentic revelation of God's Word, this motive is distinguished by its integral and radical character. That is, it penetrates to the root of created reality. As the Creator, God reveals himself as the absolute and integral origin of all things. No self-sufficient, equally primordial power stands over against him. For this reason, no expression of a dualistic principle of origin can be found within the created cosmos and equally less is it correct to discern in philosophy and the special sciences a way to the good, to the meaning of life, as the path to salvation – by escaping from one area of creation in order to move to another one. This can be done, for example, by moving to rationality, to happiness, to the collective whole (the nation, the state or the church), or to freedom and autonomy.

Yet a biblical perspective does not localize evil in a specific area of creation, but in the apostate direction of the human heart, while salvation is equally a directional matter. When the distinctness of *structure* and *direction* is disregarded an over-evaluation of a well-created part of reality ensues leading to a depreciation of something else within it. Idolizing or deifying something within creation brings honour, meant for the Creator, to a creature. The reformational philosopher, Al Wolters, succinctly characterizes this structure-direction distinction: "It is in this feature of traditional philosophy, which I have called the 'metaphysical soteriology' (and which has been blunted but not completely eradicated, in most Christian philosophies) that its religious nature comes most clearly to the fore. In my view, it ought to be a mark of philosophy which seeks to be as radical as the Bible that it renounces this whole enterprise, and simply accepts, as a point of departure, that every creature of God is good, and that sin and salvation are matters of opposing religious direction, not of good and evil sectors of the created order. All aspects of created life and reality are in principle equally good, and all are in principle equally subject to perversion and renewal" (compare 1 Timothy 4:4: "For everything God created is good").

Before we explain some implications of Dooyeweerd's idea of the creation order we still have to provide a brief analysis of the ground-motives of medieval Scholasticism and modern Humanism.

The scholastic motive of nature and grace

In his large work, *Civitas Dei* (The city of God), Augustine distinguishes between divine law and natural law. On the one hand, he accounts for the biblical distinction between the kingdom of God and the kingdom of darkness but, owing to the influence of neo-Platonism, on the other, he adds to it an un-biblical twist. As a mere *copy* of the city of God, the earthly state is negatively portrayed as *Babylon*, while its monarch is designated as *Diabolus*. This exerted a significant influence upon the subsequent struggle between church and state during the Middle Ages, particularly because both the city of God and the earthly state were regarded as all-of-life-encompassing entities. This explains why both the Greek *polis* and the *Holy Roman Empire* were still appreciated in the Aristotelian perspective of an all-encompassing, self-sufficient community (*societas perfecta*).

In the thought of Thomas Aquinas, the lower societal communities have a relative autonomy but, nonetheless, still function as *parts* of a larger *whole*. This continues the Aristotelian view which embraces all branches of society according to the mutual relationship of a *means* to an *end*, of *matter* to *form*. What is new in the conception of Thomas Aquinas is that the state merely serves as the *lower portal* for the church. While the state ought to bring its citizens to their highest *temporal* fulfillment, namely *moral perfection*, the church, as supranatural institute of *grace*, aims at *eternal bliss* (*ad finem beatutidinis aeterna*). This hierarchical relation between *nature* and *grace* is, therefore, reflected in the distinction between *lex naturalis* (a natural law which, in a *cosmic* sense, also embraces human beings in their rational-moral nature) and a divine law (*lex divina*) belonging to a supra-natural realm. In his work on the governance of the rulers, even *cities* and *provinces* are designated as *perfect communities*. The scholastic view of the relationship between *nature* and *grace* was conceived in terms of the Greek understanding of *matter* and *form*. Already in his Inaugural Address (1926), Dooyeweerd quotes the Latin slogan employed by Thomas Aquinas: *Gratia naturam non tollit, sed perficit* (grace does not disturb nature, but perfects it).

Moreover, Thomas Aquinas subscribes to the view that natural law is valid for all times and places. He states that "natural law needs no promulgation" and that the "binding force of law extends even to the future." By and large, he continues the Greek understanding of law. In a broad sense, justice embraces the moral virtues but, in a *restricted sense*, it continues to serve as one of the four moral virtues (in addition to *wisdom*, *temperance* and *courage*). Justice "tributes" to a person what legally belongs to that person, thus providing the background of the modern meaning of the jural as *(re-)tribution*. Thomas Aquinas also continues the Aristotelian distinction between *commutative* and *distributive* justice – with equality respectively viewed in terms of an *arithmetical* and a *geometrical* yardstick. In addition to *commutative* and *distributive* justice, he adds *legal justice* (*iustitia legalis*). This form of justice assigns particular legal duties to a person (among which military service). Natural law forms the basis of all positive law – when a positive legal stipulation contradicts natural law, it loses its legal validity. Objective natural law (valid for humanity as a whole) can be derived from the teleological ethical basic principle: "Do what is good and avoid what is bad". Subjective natural law includes those legal competencies that belong to a person by virtue of objective natural law (such as the right on life, integrity, acquisition of property, and so on). As encompassing virtue, general justice à la Aristotle has to direct all the other virtues towards the communal good (*bonum commune*).

Ultimately, Thomas Aquinas wanted to synthesize the Aristotelian *lex naturalis* (with its dual teleological order) with certain fundamental biblical motives. The result was that the

Aristotelian-Thomistic view denatured the meaning of law. It is merely a means in service of the goal of the moral perfection of being human, as the stepping stone towards eternal (supranatural) bliss. Therefore, the good, in a dual sense (regarding temporal moral perfection and eternal bliss), continues to incorporate all of society completely within the state and the church. This embodied the ecclesiastical unified medieval culture.

The humanistic ground-motive of nature and freedom

This entire edifice of Thomas Aquinas soon had to face new developments and challenges during the 13th and 14th centuries. Dante relativized the power claims of the church and advanced the idea of a just world-monarch who actually should be God, although he still maintained the dualism between nature and grace (philosophy and theology). But then it was, as Windelband phrased it, "the very faithful sons of the church who once again widened the split between philosophy and theology and finally made it unbridgeable." This period witnessed the emergence of what became known as the nominalistic movement which introduced the idea of the arbitrariness of the human will as well as the idea of popular sovereignty as source of law – this ultimately generated totalitarian theories of the power state (the unlimited power of the general will).

Nominalism denies any universality outside the human mind and, therefore, undermined the meaning of both law and morality, for ultimately it does not leave room for supra-individual (normative) standards of conduct. In his *Sententien*, Ockham advanced the view that universality "is only in the soul and therefore not in the things".

In his treatise on the method according to which a correct use of our understanding ought to be made Descartes mentions that he was particularly pleased with mathematics owing to its certainty and the self-evidence of its argumentations. The method developed by Descartes is subdivided into four steps with analysis (into the finest details) and reconstructing the more complex occupying the centre. As criterion of truth Descartes employs the general rule: whatever is clearly and distinctly perceived (*percipio*) is true. However, what guarantees the nature of (true) knowledge?

As guarantee Descartes introduces his "idea" of God. The idea of God as an infinite, eternal, immutable, independent, omniscient and all-powerful substance is the clearest of all the idea in my understanding. Since I am finite, so Descartes continues his argument, this idea of God – God therefore does exist – must be generated by God in my thinking (*Meditationes*, III). Since God cannot mislead us, it is clear that the certainty and truth of all science and knowledge is dependent upon the true God, insofar that I cannot obtain proper knowledge of anything else unless I have prior knowledge of God. Descartes searches the foundation of his thought in the *cogito*. In the employment of the mathematical method it requires God as the guarantor of clear and distinct thinking. Thus Descartes merely uses God in order to provide certainty to his (presumed clear and distinct) deified mathematical thinking and at once the new mathematical method acquires the stamp of infallibility.

Yet Descartes wanted to maintain the ideal of a free and autonomous personality (the humanistic personality ideal) by strictly distinguishing the thinking substance from the body as extended substance.

Hobbes carries the mathematical science ideal so radically through that he even considers the soul merely as a mechanism of feeling motions. Leibniz in particular elaborated the science ideal further, stimulated by the discovery of the differential and integral calculus (the so-called infinitesimal calculus).

A psychologistic turn emerges in the development of the science ideal when Locke, in his *Essay concerning Human Understanding*, partially binds the contents of thought to the simple (elementary) sensory representations ("ideas"). However, from the elementary sensory impressions thought can operate freely and actively in order to arrive at compound representations. The distinction drawn by Locke between empirical factual knowledge and the necessary relations between concepts, as well as his introduction of intuition as basis of exact scientific knowledge (as found in the demonstrations of mathematics) created a split in his psychologistic intentions, for with the aid of the mathematical method of proof mathematics and ethics can provide us with apriori knowledge and infallible certainty.

In a consistent psychologistic fashion Berkeley leaves behind the distinction between primary and secondary qualities (amongst others still defended by Locke). In line with his thesis that to be is to be perceived (*esse est percipi*) Berkeley only acknowledges the reality of secondary (psychic) qualities.

Subsequently Hume carried the science ideal to its ultimate consequences by reducing all facets of reality to the basic denominator of perception. "To hate, to love, to think, to feel, to see; all this is nothing but to perceive." According to Hume "all our ideas or more feeble perceptions" are mere "copies of our impressions," while there are only three principles of connection between ideas, namely resemblance, contiguity in time and space, and cause and effect.

Hume reduced the assumed universality of the law of causality to a psychic law of association by connecting it in a remarkable way with habit and faith: "after a repetition of similar instances, the mind is carried by habit, upon the appearance of one event, to expect its usual attendant, and to believe that it will exist." Since habit in itself is not an impression but solely serves the mutual connection of impressions in the order of cause and effect it is understandable why Hume introduces it with an appeal to a universal "a principle of human nature, which is universally acknowledged, and which is well known by its effects." In this section Hume even calls custom "the great guide of human life."

The crucial problem for this psychologism is to account for *constancy* amidst psychical becoming and change. Arbitrariness and chance pose an unsolvable problem for the psychologistic science ideal – and Hume did not provide an answer to these questions.

If all of reality in the final analysis is reduced to a mathematical, kinematic (compare Newton's physics), physical or psychical denominator, no room is left for the humanistic faith in the (ethical) freedom and autonomy of a person. These consequences of the developing science ideal explains why Kant, in the Preface to the second edition of his *Kritik der reinen Vernunft* (*Critique of Pure Reason* – CPR) declares that he had to restrict knowing (science) in order to make room for faith: "I have therefore found it necessary to deny knowledge, in order to make room for faith" ("Ich musste also das Wissen aufheben, um zum Glauben Platz zu bekommen").

Dooyeweerd and Kant

In the first volume of his *A New Critique of Theoretical Thought*, Dooyeweerd substantiated this insight by means of a penetrating analysis of the place of Kant within the dialectical development of modern philosophy.

With Hume, Kant accepts that all knowledge commences with (sensory) experience (CPR B,1). However, this does not entail that all knowledge is derived from experience for there must be just as much a contribution from our capacity of knowing. In order to explain this, Kant explains his distinction between apriori and aposteriori: knowledge that is independent from our experience and from sensory impressions is called apriori as distinct from knowledge derived aposteriori from experience (B,2). Kant furthermore distinguishes between analytic and synthetic judgements: if the relation between the subject and predicate of a statement is such that the predicate belongs to what is contained in the subject, such a statement is analytic, if not, it is synthetic (B,10). In the light of these distinctions Kant formulates the general task of pure reason, given in the question: How are synthetical judgments apriori possible? ("Wie sind synthetische Urteile apriori möglich?").

Since, according to Kant, all theoretical sciences contain synthetical judgments *apriori*, the question concerning the possibility of such judgments first of all must be applied to pure mathematics (*reine Mathematik*) and pure physics (*reine Naturwissenschaft*) (B,20).

Subsequently Kant immediately raises the question regarding metaphysics (flowing from the nature of reason) and then focuses on the problem of delimiting pure reason. A critique of pure reason cannot stop at the merely natural inclination to metaphysics, generating questions that cannot be answered by any use of reason bound to experience (or to principles derived from it), for inevitably this leads to contradictions. Rather the question ought to be asked if pure reason could be stretched beyond all limits or whether it is not rather the case that clear and determinate boundaries for it ought to be found.

It boils down to the question how metaphysics as a science is possible. (That is to say, regarding the question: how are synthetical judgments *apriori* possible in metaphysics?)

In the *Transzendentale Asthetik* Kant commences by isolating sensibility so that everything added by the concepts of understanding is separated, entailing that nothing remains but pure intuition (*Anschauung*). The receptive faculty through which we acquire representations of objects is known as sensibility and through it we obtain intuitions (*Anschauungen*). In the isolation of sensibility even whatever belongs to sensation (*Empfindung*) must be separated so that pure intuition and the mere form of phenomena remains, that is to say that solely that remains which sensibility *apriori* can supply.

In this explanation we encounter the term appearances (*Erscheinungen*) which certainly already contains the basic problem of Kant's thought. According to Kant it follows naturally from the concept of an *appearance* that it is correlated with something that in itself is *not* an appearance, something that must be an object independent of sensibility. What is designated as external objects are mere representations of our sensibility that have as correlate *Things-in-Themselves*.

This innocent appeal to that which apparently flows in a natural way (*natürlicher Weise*) from the concept of an appearance, when subjected to closer scrutiny reveals a direct connection with Kant's problem of demarcation: in order to safe-guard human freedom and faith, Kant restricted science.

These distinctions in the thought of Kant reveal the directing role of the humanistic basic motive of *nature* and *freedom* (*science ideal* and *personality ideal*). The different ways in which the term *transcendental* is employed in the philosophy of Kant and in the thought of Dooyeweerd illustrates their distinct ultimate commitments.

Dooyeweerd positions this term within his non-reductionist ontology (irreducible sphere-sovereign modal aspects and individuality-structures), aimed at giving an account of the ontic order underlying and making possible our richly varied but coherent experience of reality.

Dooyeweerd's view is informed by the biblical creation motive and directed by the ontic principle of the excluded antinomy. The latter principle unmasks the shortcomings present in all attempts to reduce the diversity within creation to one or another deified perspective.

In Dooyeweerd's philosophy the term *transcendental* therefore reveals his *ontic* intention.

In the philosophy of Kant, by contrast, the use of the term *transcendental* is motivated by the dialectical motive of nature and freedom. We noted that it surfaces in the context of distinguishing between *essence* (*Ding-an-sich*) and *appearance*. Since the initial science ideal reduced all of reality to a causal determination, Kant had to restrict the science ideal to appearances in order to safe-guard a supra-sensory domain of (practical-ethical) human freedom. But his focus is on (*apriori*) conditions of possibility inherent in the knowing human subject. This explains why he does not employ the term *transcendental* in an *ontic* sense, but rather in a subject-oriented (epistemic or cognitive) sense. The Kantian transcendental (*apriori*) forms rest on two epistemic stems, *sensibility* (with space and time as outward and inward forms of intuition), and *understanding* (with its twelve categories). In the second edition of his CPR he states: "I call all knowledge transcendental which is not also concerned with objects, *but with our mode of knowing objects, insofar as this could be possible apriori.*" Occasionally this work also employs the term transcendental in the sense of *exceeding the limits of experience*: "The basic statements of pure understanding, … ought merely to be empirical and not transcendental, i.e. stretching beyond the limits of experience in its employment."

Kant considers the *freedom* of the human soul as a *Ding-an-sich* and then remarks that "there is no contradiction in supposing that one and the same will is, in the appearance, that is, in its visible acts, necessarily subject to the law of nature, and so far not free, while yet, as belonging to a thing in itself, it is not subject to that law, and is therefore free". The link between the distinction of *Ding-an-sich* and *appearance* on the one hand and its rootedness in the basic motive of nature and freedom, is evinced in the following quotations from the 1787 edition of Kant's CPR.

> The common but fallacious presupposition of the absolute reality of appearances here manifests its injurious influence, to the confounding of reason. For if appearances are things in themselves, *freedom cannot be upheld* (my italics – DS).

On the next page the basic motive of Kant's whole CPR is clear:

> My purpose has only been to point out that since the thorough-going connection of all appearances, in a context of nature, is an inexorable law, the inevitable consequence of obstinately insisting on the reality of appearances is to destroy all freedom. Those who thus follow the common view have never been able to reconcile *nature* and *freedom* (I am italicizing – DS).

The upshot was that Kant, in the final analysis,

settled for two domains – the "nature concept" and the "freedom concept" – which are totally separated by the large *abyss* dividing what is supra-sensory from appearances ("... durch die große Kluft, welche das Übersinnliche von den Erscheinungen trent, ganzlich abgesondert"). For Kant this concerns the opposing elements of theoretical reason and practical reason which ultimately simply reinforces the basic dualism between natural necessity and super-sensory freedom – each with its own lawgiver.

The difference between the biblical motive of creation and its secularized counter-part in the thought of Kant is best seen in the claim made in his *Prolegomena* (1783), namely that human understanding is the *formal law-giver of nature*, for according to him it does not derive its laws *from* nature, but prescribes them *to* nature: "understanding creates its laws (apriori) not out of nature, but prescribes them to nature."

Post-Kantian philosophy

After Kant romanticism (Herder, Goethe) facilitated the rise of the German freedom idealism (Schelling, Hegel and Fichte) which gave full primacy the personality ideal. But soon the science ideal acquired primacy again in the thought of Maimon, Comte, Marx, Darwin and Haeckel. By the end of the 19th century and beginning of the 20th century two neo-Kantian schools dominated the philosophical scene, namely the Marburgh school (science ideal primacy – Cohen, Cassirer, Natorp, Lask, and Kelsen) and the Baden school (giving primacy once more to the personality ideal – Windelband, Rickert, and Weber). During the first decades of the 20th century multiple philosophical trends emerged: the personalism of Buber (struggling with the dualism of nature and freedom); the legacy of Wittgenstein, partly elaborated in the logical atomism of Russell and in ordinary language philosophy (Ryle) and analytical philosophy in general (by and large in the grip of a physicalist science ideal); neo-Marxism (reverting to the freedom motive – Bloch and the Frankfurt school – Adorno, Horkheimer and Habermas); positivism reinforcing the science ideal (Mach), continued in the neo-positivism of Ayer, Carnap, Schlick, Hempel, Hahn; while the phenomenology of Husserl advocated a distinct transcendental intuitionistic science ideal; Existentialism reverted to the primacy of the freedom motive (Heidegger, Sartre, and Jaspers), and postmodernism elaborated an irrationalistic and historicistic variant of the personality ideal. The inherent dialectic of the two poles of nature and freedom, mutually presupposing and threatening each other, is perhaps best captured by Jaspers in his work *Philosophie* (1948): "While freedom is only through and against nature, it must of necessity fail" ("Weil Freiheit nur durch und gegen Natur ist, muss es notwendig scheitern").

We may now turn to the basic structure of Dooyeweerd's philosophy.

The Basic Contours of Dooyeweerd's Philosophy

DISTINGUISHING BETWEEN Creator and creation precludes all attempts at deifying anything or any aspect within creation. Whatever there is within creation is subject to God-given laws. The cosmic law-order embraces the central religious dimension of reality (the domain of ultimate commitments and ground-motives), the dimension of cosmic time, the dimension of modal aspects and the dimension of individuality-structures (the type laws or structural principles of natural and social entities).

A summarized analysis will now be given of Dooyeweerd's original and penetrating *Reformational Philosophy*.

The theory of modal law-spheres

Whereas concrete (natural and social) entities correspond to the "what" question, modal aspects are accessible through the "how" question. From Latin we inherited expressions such as *modus operandi* and *modus vivendi* in which the *how* is represented by the term "modus." An aspect is therefore a specific (unique) mode of reality. In a general sense it is a *modus quo* or a *mode of being*. It provides a framework within which everything and all processes within reality function. As an equivalent for referring to facets, aspects or functions, one can therefore also speak about *modalities*, *modal aspects* or *modal functions*.

Subject functions and object functions

Suppose a person is not quite sure of whether she is observing a chair, then the natural question will be: *what* is this? Once it is certain that a *chair* is noticed, multiple *how* questions could ensue, such as *how* many legs does it have? *how* big is it? *how* strong is it? *how* expensive is it? and so on. The dimension of the "*how*" is irreducible to the "*what*." When entities and processes are resolved into functions we meet *functionalism*; and when modal functions are treated as if they are entities they are *reified* ("hypostatized"). Claiming that everything is number (the Pythagoreans) or that everything is physical (modern physicalism) are examples of *functionalist* approaches. The habit of referring to the origin of *life* represents a reificatory mode of speech, because it treats an aspect (the biotic) as if it is an entity. Living entities certainly do have a biotic function, but their existence exceeds the boundaries of their biotic functioning. This is evident from the fact that all living entities are founded in typical physico-chemical constellations (of atoms, molecules and macro-molecules) – and no biologist or physicist can deny that atoms and molecules are not alive (the largest macro-molecule is about a million times smaller than the smallest living cell).

Modal aspects belong to a dimension of reality that is different from (natural and societal) entities and events. For this reason the universal functional structure of modal aspects condition the existence of all concrete entities.

Material things, plants and animals as well as human beings, in principle function in all aspects of reality. But only human beings function actively, i.e., as subjects, in all aspects of reality. While material things have subject functions in the first four modal aspects (number, space, the kinematic and the physical), plants furthermore are also subjects in the biotic aspect and animals, as sentient creatures, in addition are subjects within the sensitive mode. Material things have object functions in the aspects succeeding the physical aspect. Plants have object functions within the post-biotic aspects and animals within the post-sensitive aspects.

Insofar as physical entities are material, they are not objects but *subjects* (subject to quantitative, spatial, kinematic and physical laws), and insofar as they are objects, they hold this status because they are considered according to one or another post-physical trait – for example, as something perceived (sense-object), as something analyzed (identified and distinguished from something else – logical-analytical object), as something bought or sold (economic object), and so on. Therefore, although material things could be *objectified* by humans, this objectification presupposes their primary existence as (physical) *subjects*. Speaking of them in all possible contexts as "objects" simply accentuates the powerful *subjectivistic* (human-centred) legacy in Western thinking.

The multi-aspectual nature of human beings

Within the quantitative aspect the human being functions as a *unity*. We can count human beings for there are many of them. The particular form and shape of our bodies highlight the concrete function we have within the aspect of space. Human beings can move – even when they are sitting or lying they share in the movement of the earth around its axis and around the sun ("rest" is therefore relative, it is a "state of motion"). The strength of our bodies (or muscles) brings to expression our function within the physical aspect of energy-operation. Of course we are alive (biotic function) and are sensitive (sensory mode). We have the analytical ability to identify and distinguish. Furthermore, we are culturally active (thus functioning within the cultural-historical aspect), we use language (our function within the sign mode), interact with other human beings in social contexts (our social functioning) and we can buy and sell stuff (economic function). In addition we appreciate what is beautiful or ugly (aesthetic mode), legal or illegal (jural mode), moral or immoral (ethical mode) and trustworthy or not (fiduciary, certitudinal or faith mode).

Retrocipations and anticipations on the law side and factual side

Dooyeweerd distinguishes within each aspect a law side or norm side and a factual side, where the latter embraces both subject functions and object functions. For example, the arithmetical laws of addition and multiplication determine and delimit natural numbers – adding or multiplying any two of them always once more yields other natural numbers. The law of subtraction is not closed over the natural numbers, because subtracting 12 from 7 yields a negative number, namely –5. Therefore recognizing another numerical law turns out to be correlated with additional subjects at the factual side of this aspect, designated as the *integers*. Likewise, discerning division (the inverse of multiplication) on the law side of this aspect also requires new correlating subjects at the factual side, namely *fractions*.

Within the quantitative aspect there are no modal objects, only arithmetical subjects. Applying the just-mentioned quantitative laws therefore solely holds for numerical subject-subject relations. Surely, within the spatial aspect there are also subject-subject relations, such as intersecting lines. But this is the first aspect in which there are subject-object relations as well.

Whereas a spatial subject is always factually extended in some *dimension* (such as a *one*-dimensional line, a *two*-dimensional area, and so on), a *spatial object* solely serves as a boundary (in a delimiting way). The boundaries of a determined line-stretch are the two *points* delimiting it (with the line as a one-dimensional spatial subject). But these boundary points themselves are not extended in one dimension. Within one dimension, points are therefore not spatial subjects, but merely *spatial objects*, dependent upon the factual extension of the line. Yet a line may serve in a similar delimiting way within two dimensions – for the lines delimiting an area are not extended themselves in a two-dimensional sense.

These remarks presuppose the idea of the uniqueness (modal sphere-sovereignty) of each modal aspect and the inter-modal connections between them, designated by Dooyeweerd as backward-pointing analogies (retrocipations) and forward-pointing analogies (anticipations).

In the ontic order of aspects the numerical aspect precedes the spatial aspect. Within the former one therefore finds anticipations to the spatial aspect and within the latter there are retrocipations to the numerical aspect. Speaking of 1, 2, or 3 dimensions within the aspect of space analogically reflect the original quantitative meaning of the natural numbers 1, 2, and 3. The numbers indicate an order of extension and there they appear on the law side of the spatial aspect.

Distance appears at the factual side of the spatial aspect and points back to the numerical mode because it is specified by providing a *number*. Therefore it represents a retrocipatory analogy within space. A line is therefore *not* the "shortest distance between two points." Distance here is the *measure* of extension, not the extension itself. [At the second international conference of mathematics, held in Paris in 1900, David Hilbert included, as the fourth of the 23 "Mathematische Problemen" which he discussed, the "Problem of the straight line as the shortest *connection* (*Verbindung*) of two points." It is reprinted in Hilbert 1970.]

The numerical time order of succession on the law side of the numerical aspect reveals the most basic meaning of infinity, in the literal sense of *endlessness* (without an end – the *successive infinite*). It is only when the meaning of number is deepened through an anticipatory analogy, pointing towards the spatial time order of simultaneity (in the sense of *at once*) that we meet the idea of *infinite totalities* (employing the idea of the *at once infinite*). [Since Aristotle these two forms of the infinite are designated as the potential and actual infinite. Interestingly Dooyeweerd rejected the actual infinite by following the intuitionistic mathematicians Brouwer and Weyl, without realizing that his own theory of modal aspects provides a sound account for the employment of the at once infinite.]

The infinite divisibility of any (factually extended) spatial subject, by contrast, refers back to the law side of the numerical aspect where we noted the order of arithmetical succession in its primitive meaning of endlessness. The continuous extension of any spatial subject embodies the original factual meaning of the *spatial whole-parts relation* which entails a retrocipation to the successive infinite on the law side of the numerical aspect with its implied *infinite divisibility*. The *interval* within the system of rational numbers analogically reflects this infinite divisibility of a spatial subject and the latter, as we have just pointed out, represents a retrocipation from space to the primitive meaning of the successive infinite on the law side of the numerical aspect.

One implication of the retrocipatory and anticipatory analogies within the structure of modal aspects is that every special science has to account for the specific meaning in which these analogical elements are employed. Let us now illustrate this point with reference to Dooyeweerd's field of special scientific expertise, the science of law, delimited by the jural aspect:

Aspects	Retrocipations and Anticipations
Faith aspect	Jural/legal certainty trust)
Ethical aspect	Jural/legal morality (fault, good faith, etc.)
Jural aspect	[Meaning-nucleus: retribution]
Aesthetic aspect	Jural/legal harmony
Economic aspect	Jural/legal economy (avoiding excess)
Social aspect	Jural/legal interaction
Lingual aspect	Jural/legal signification and interpretation

Cultural-historical aspect	Jural power / Legal competence
Logical-analytical aspect	Jural lawfulness and unlawfulness (consistency)
Sensory aspect	Jural/legal sensitivity (intention, will)
Biotical aspect	Jural/legal life
Physical aspect	Jural/legal dynamics (causality)
Kinematic aspect	Jural/legal constancy/movement (transfer, conveyance)
Spatial aspect	Jural/legal sphere, jurisdiction, ambit
Arithmetical aspect	Jural/legal order (unity & multiplicity)

The core meaning of an aspect resides in its meaning-nucleus which guarantees its uniqueness, irreducibility and indefinability. Dooyeweerd holds that the core primitive (indefinable) elements characteristic of the uniqueness of each aspect are embedded within the general modal structure of these aspects. His theory conjectures that every unique modal (functional) aspect therefore has a meaning-nucleus that qualifies all analogical references to other aspects. At the factual side of the various aspects one finds subject-subject and subject-object relations that are correlated with and subject to the law-side of each aspect (also expressed in the correlation of *time order* and *time duration*).

The general structure of a modal aspect embraces the following features.

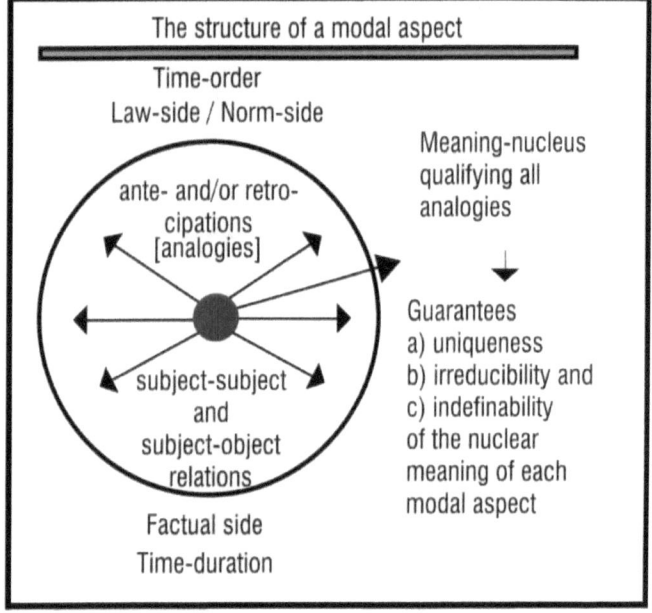

Since the meaning-nucleus of an aspect is *indefinable* every attempt to define it terminates in a tautology, in a reduction (which is antinomous) or simply misses the target. The indefinable terms are *primitive terms*.

Primitive terms

According to Yourgrau Gödel "insisted that to know the primitive concepts, one must not only understand their relationships to the other primitives but must grasp them on their own, by a kind of 'intuition'." It should be noted, however, that this statement does not realize that primitive terms are not primitive concepts. We need a *word* (a 'primitive term') to *designate* our *intuitive insight*, but the latter exceeds the limits of *concepts*. Accepting that there are primitive terms avoids an infinite regress and requires an intuitive insight based upon what is evident.

The gifted German mathematician, David Hilbert, believed that it will be possible to provide a formal *proof* for the consistency and completeness of an axiomatic system in mathematics, but the youthful genius of Gödel, at the age of 25, ruined this dream in 1931. Hilbert died in 1943 and three years later his student, Hermann Weyl (1946), wrote (with a view to the outcome of Gödel's proof and the inevitability of taking into account what is evident), "It must have been hard on Hilbert, the axiomatist, to acknowledge that the insight of consistency is rather to be attained by intuitive reasoning which is based on evidence and not on axioms."

Dooyeweerd comments on the attempt of Russell (in 1903) to define the number 2 with the aid of his logical concept of a class. "1 + 1 is the number of a class -w- which is the logical sum of two classes -u- and -v- which have no common term and have each only one term." Dooyeweerd recognizes the vicious circle in this definition, for in order to arrive at the number 2 Russell had to use this number to distinguish the TWO (!) classes u and v. Dooyeweerd remarks that "for the simple distinction of the classes he needs number in its original meaning of quantity" – clearly a circular argument.

Hilbert is therefore correct by emphasizing in 1913 that logic and arithmetic cannot analyze their respective fields of investigation without acknowledging the interconnections between these domains. He states:

> Only when we analyze attentively do we realize that in presenting the laws of logic we already have had to employ certain arithmetical basic concepts, for example the concept of a set and partially also the concept of number, particularly as cardinal number [*Anzahl*]. Here we end up in a vicious circle and in order to avoid paradoxes it is necessary to come to a partially simultaneous development of the laws of logic and arithmetic.

The legal scholar, Leo Polak, tried to define the meaning of the jural as follows: "Retribution is an objective, trans egoistic, harmonization of interests." In the *Systematic Volume* of his *Encyclopedia of the Science of Law* Dooyeweerd shows that this attempted definition completely misses the target:

> Polak wants to express the meaning of what is normative and law-conformative with the term 'objective'. But since every normative law-sphere has its law-side this is not at all specifying what is distinct about the meaning of retribution. The element 'trans egoistic' is derived from the meaning of neighborly love in a moral sense and therefore has a non-jural meaning. In the element 'harmonization of interests' the term 'interest' totally lacks any delineation. There

are scientific interests, social interests, economic and aesthetic interests, legal interests, and faith interests. Which one of these meanings is intended? Legal interests? But then this definition suffers from the well-known logical error that incorporates in the definition exactly that which should be determined by the definition. Finally, the word 'harmonization', in so far as it is used without any modal qualification, is related to the meaning-nucleus of the aesthetic aspect which is only analogically reflected in the moment of a jural harmonization of interests. The retributive mode therefore has to qualify this moment, but could never be qualified by it. The result is a general concept fully lacking any delimitation. It could just as well be seen as a moral rule regarding the distribution of alms.

The elementary basic concepts of the academic disciplines

Special scientists tend to think that their own discipline employs concepts that are peculiar to that specific discipline. This explains why some scholars on the one hand want to get away from certain "misleading" figures or metaphors, but on the other want to demarcate a unique and if possible even exclusive universe of discourse.

The sociologist Fichter (1968), for example, discards "organic metaphors" and he even claims that *analogies* are *dispensible*. Yet he continues by analyzing the problem of *constants*. The term *constancy*, however, originally belongs to the domain of the *kinematic aspect* of *uniform (constant) motion*. The implication is that it could only be used by other disciplines in a *non-original* way, that is, in an *analogical* fashion. Fichter believes that what he considers as basic concepts represent "constant and everywhere appearing elements." But Fichter does not realize that the term "everywhere" derives from the spatial aspect of reality. Just consider the equivalent spatial term: *universal*. Similarly, the term "elements" reflects the unique meaning of the quantitative aspect, since it is related to the meaning of *multiplicity*: the *one and the many*. This implies that Fichter necessarily had to use numerical and spatial terms in order to explain his employment of the (kinematic) term *constancy*.

What has happened here is that the analysis of the elementary basic concepts of a special science could only be accomplished by implicitly or explicitly using other (*analyzed* or *not yet analyzed*) analogical structural moments within the modal structure of the aspect concerned.

It should not surprise us that Fichter, on the basis of his introduction of "social constants," speaks of *social dynamics* and *social change* and a few pages further also about *social causes*. However, the relation between *cause* and effect in the first place manifests itself within the structure of the *physical* aspect of reality. Analogous to this physical relation, sociology employs the (analogical basic) concept of social causation (in 1942 MacIver wrote a book on this issue). In other words, although Fichter believes that he can dispense with the former "imaginative analogies" used by sociologists through the development of an "own terminology," he continues (albeit unconsciously and unintentionally) to use certain analogical concepts – including those from the biotic aspect (such as the phrase: "social life").

In his *Encyclopedia of the Science of Law* Dooyeweerd lists the elementary basic concepts analyzed in this systematic volume:

> legal norm, legal subject and legal object, legal fact, subjective right and legal duty, area of validity and the locus of a legal fact, lawfulness and unlawfulness, jural attribution and accountability, jural will, jural causality (legal ground, legal consequence as to the law side; the subjective or objective causality of, respectively, a legal transaction or objective legal fact, as to the subject-side), jural positivizing and the originating jural form (formal source of law), legal organ and jural competence (legal power), jural interpretation and legal significance, jural fault or guilt, good morals, good faith.

Once the elementary basic concepts have been analyzed, one has to proceed to an analysis of the compound or complex basic concepts of a discipline.

The compound basic concepts of the academic disciplines

The compound basic concepts of a discipline incorporate multiple elementary basic concepts *at once*. In his *Encyclopedia of the Science of Law* Dooyeweerd proceeds with an analysis of compound basic concepts such as legal subject, legal object, subjective right, jural norms and so on.

As an example we shall explain how Dooyeweerd's approach enables us to articulate the concept of a (natural) law and a norm (principle).

Intrinsic to the notion of a natural law is the nature of an *order for*. This makes an appeal to the *unity* in the *multiplicity* of different natural laws, for without such unity there will be a clash of laws, abolishing the possibility of an *order of laws*. The constitutive role of the numerical mode is clear in this concept of *order*. Furthermore, a law entails its correlate, namely that which is *factually subjected* to it – this insight entails the inherent universal scope of a law which is dependent upon the spatial notion of *everywhere* (at all places). Without the spatial (dimensional) distinction between above and below, the assumed correlation of law and subject does not make any sense. That the validity of a natural law is not something incidental is captured by acknowledging its constancy which demonstrates the constitutive role of the *kinematic* mode in our understanding of a natural law. The notion of *validity* (being in force) derives from the core meaning of the physical aspect, and it has to be incorporated in the concept of natural law, because otherwise the ability to say that a law *determines* whatever is subjected to it would collapse.

The compound or complex basic concept of a *natural law* may therefore be formulated by incorporating terms from number, space, the kinematic as well as the physical aspects:

> As a unique, distinct, and universally valid order for what is factually correlated with and subjected to it, a natural law constantly holds (either in an unspecified way as in the case of modal laws or in a specified way as in the case of type laws) within the domain within which it conditions what is subjected to it.

Regarding the nature of *norms* or *principles* Dooyeweerd faced two extremes. The one option is to claim universal validity for normative principles *per se*. Alternatively one may deny that there are no universal or constant starting points for human action since all positive decisions by human beings are *variable* (changeful). Traditional theories of *natural law* chose the first option, while *legal positivism* opted for the second.

Dooyeweerd's successor at the Free University, H.J. Hommes, succinctly characterizes the traditional concept of natural law in his dissertation (1961) as follows:

> Natural law in its traditional sense is the totality of pre-positive legal norms (not brought into existence through a human declaration of will in the formation of law) that are immutable, universal and per se valid as well as the eventual subjective natural rights and correlating duties, based upon a natural order (whether or not traced back to a divine origin), such that the human being can derive it from the natural order

aided by natural reason.

However, at the beginning of the 19th century legal positivism received its most powerful ally in modern (post-Enlightenment) *historicism*. In 1815 Von Savigny wrote, in the first Volume of the newly established Journal for Historical Legal Science (*Zeitschrift für geschichtliche Rechtswissenschaft*), that law is a purely historical phenomenon and that next to or above positive law, there is no immutable and eternal legal system of natural law.

In order to transcend the mutual exclusivity of these two positions Dooyeweerd realized that an acknowledgement of *ontic normativity* is required. Such norming ontic points of departure are not the *result* of human intervention and construction, since they lie at the basis of all human shaping and construction. Normative contraries, such as logical – illogical, polite – impolite, frugal – wasteful, legal – illegal and so on depend upon universal, constant starting points (principles). Although there may be disagreement about the meaning of analysis, of sociation, of economizing or of pursuing justice, the reality of the mentioned contraries affirm the underlying normative structuredness of these human capacities. This understanding of principles transcends the subjectivistic inclination of modern philosophy insofar as it accepts the existence of normative principles in a truly ontic-transcendental sense. This perspective opposes both the rationalistic position of natural law and the irrationalistic stance shared by different trends of legal positivism.

Once the implicit assumption of human autonomy is questioned, it becomes clear that our human experience of legal relationships and our human sense of justice are not the product of individual or collective (rational) construction, since whatever we can observe within the domain of legal relationships (and other spheres of normativity) is founded in and made possible by the normative structure of the jural (and other) aspect(s) of reality. An investigation into what makes possible every positive form of our normed experience of reality, proceeds in what may be called a *transcendental-empirical method*.

The legacy of natural law discerned an element of the underlying (universal, constant) structure of our legal experience, but it distorted its meaning by assuming that those underlying principles have already been *made valid* (*enforced*) for all times and all places. Yet no principle in this fundamental ontic sense is valid *per se*. Every principle requires *human intervention* in order to be made valid, i.e. no (pre-positive) ontic principle holds by and of itself. Only human beings are able to *enforce* them and only human beings can give a positive form or shape to them. Different schools of thought designate the result of giving form to underlying principles as *positivizations* (we mention Habermas, Smend and Hartmann).

Historicism, by contrast, is justified in questioning the metaphysical idea of *immutable* and *eternal principles of natural law* that are (supposed to be) valid *per se*. But its emphasis on the supposedly intrinsically *changefulness* of *historical* reality collapses the normative meaning of law and justice into an anchorless *relativism*. In legal practice, it results in a merely formal account that actually sanctions putting any arbitrary content in the form of law.

Dooyeweerd is therefore justified in rejecting the position assumed by Kelsen, who holds in his *Reine Rechtslehre* (*Pure Theory of Law* – 1960) that "every arbitrary content can be law. There exists no human action for which, according to its quality, it is excluded from being the content of a legal norm."

Without an insight into the foundational relation between constancy and change (dynamics) no sound account of normativity will be possible. Historicism and postmodernism emphasizes change at the *cost* of constancy, instead of realizing that change can only be detected on the basis of constancy.

The modern ideal of autonomous freedom (exemplified, amongst others, in the thought of Rousseau, Kant and Rawls) actually reifies the freedom of human subjects to give positive form or positivize pre-positive jural (and other) normative principles. Without the recognition of such (universal and constant) principles, dependent on human intervention for making them valid, the extremes of natural law and historicism cannot be avoided.

The first three modal points of entry are sufficient to characterize the nature of a prepositive (i.e., not-yet-positivized) principle. In this sense every principle serves as a universal, constant starting point for human action – clearly employing terms derived from the numerical (starting point), spatial (universal) and kinematic (constant) aspects. When the scope of our analysis is expanded beyond these first three modes of explanation, one can account for a principle as a compound basic concept in the following way:

> A principle is a universal, constant, starting point for human action that can only be made valid (enforced) by a competent organ with an accountable (free) will, capable of giving a positive shape to such a starting point in varying historical situations, in the light of an appropriate interpretation of the relevant circumstances, and resulting in a norm-conformative or anti-normative positivization of the principle concerned.

The challenge facing Dooyeweerd was to produce a circumscription of the concept of law (in its jural sense), both to its law side and factual side. The result of his response, found in the second volume of his *magnum opus*, *A New Critique of Theoretical Thought*. It reads as follows:

1. The modal meaning of the juridical aspect on its law-side is: the unity (the order) in the multiplicity of retributive norms positivized from super-arbitrary principles and having a particular, signified meaning, area and term of validity. In the correlation of the interpersonal and

the communal functions of the competency spheres, these norms are to be imputed to the will of formative organs, and they regulate the balance in a multiplicity of interpersonal and group interests according to grounds and effects, in the coherence of permissive and prohibitive (or injunctive) functions by means of a harmonizing process preventing from any excess, in the meaning nucleus of retribution.

2. The modal meaning of the juridical aspect on its subject-side is the multiplicity of the factual retributive subject-object relations imputable to the subjective will of subjects qualified to act, or per representation to those not so qualified. These subject-object relations are bound to a place and time, in the correlation of the communal and the interpersonal rights and duties of their subjects. In their positive meaning – in accordance with (or in conflict with) the juridical norms – these subject-object relations are causal with respect to the harmonious balance of human interests in the meaning of retribution.

Disclosure as a deepening of meaning

Whereas retrocipations are (ever-present) *constitutive* building-blocks within a modal aspect, its anticipatory analogies are dependent upon being opened up through a process of meaning disclosure. In connection with the anticipations and retrocipations between number and space it was pointed out that the primitive meaning of (numerical) infinity (endlessness) could be deepened by a numerical anticipation to the spatial whole-parts relation, incorporated in the idea of *infinite totalities*. Inherent to this opening up is the idea of the *at once infinite*. It functions as a *regulative hypothesis* within mathematical thinking. Employing the at once infinite makes it possible, for example, to hypothesize any given endless (successive infinite) sequence of numbers *as if* all the elements of such a sequence of numbers are given *at once*, as an *infinite totality*.

Consider the disclosure of the cultural-historical aspect. The normative contrary historical-unhistorical uproots the positivistic pre-occupation with historical *facts*, for without implicitly applying a historical norm of development, it would be impossible to speak of *reactionary* or *revolutionary* historical events. Reaction and revolution presuppose the normative meaning of historical constancy (continuity) and historical change – revealing on the norm side the coherence between the historical aspect and the foundational role of the kinematic and physical aspects. Reactionary movements cling to the status quo without any flexibility or willingness to face the challenge of changing historical circumstances. Revolutionary movements, by contrast, take such challenges so seriously that no room is left for any historical continuity.

It is only when a sound application of the (constitutive) norm of historical continuity prevails that constructive reformation takes place, avoiding the historically anti-normative extremes of *reaction* and *revolution*. Historical development is always confronted with a struggle between progressive and conservative forces, but only through continuity-abiding reformation is it possible to bend these opposing forces into the pathway of historical norm-conformity.

Tradition, as the guardian of historical continuity, not only embodies the worthwhile legacy of the past, but also calls for continued reformation. But when an accountable reformation takes place, it only causes changes on the basis of historical continuity and not at the cost of it.

In the context of the historical aspect, the task-setting nature of historical principles entails that the calling to (formative) control – over fellow human beings (the *competence* vested in some or other societal *office*) and over cultural objects made by humankind – comes to expression in processes conforming to or violating the fundamental principles of historical differentiation and historical integration. These principles are functional principles exhibiting the modal universality of the cultural-historical mode.

Constitutive historical principles are not eliminated when a deepening or disclosure of the meaning of the historical aspect takes place. The first element of deepening the meaning of the historical aspect is found when the awareness of what is historically significant materializes in inscriptions, monuments, written historical accounts, and so on. The latter serve as sources for the historian. The difference between what is historically significant and what is insignificant is made possible by the anticipatory coherence between the cultural-historical aspect and the sign mode. Cultures in which this anticipatory moment is not yet disclosed do not, strictly speaking, participate in world history, as Hegel realized.

Constitutive meaning-moments within the cultural-historical aspect acquire new meaning under the guidance of regulative moments. For example, an articulated understanding of what is historically significant enables a more nuanced identification of a cultural community with its historical past and at once highlights avenues through which what is fruitful in its tradition could be pursued in further historical development. Once the social anticipation is opened up, social intercourse with other cultures leads to an equally articulated development of the national identity of communities. The uniqueness and individuality of cultures are thus recognized. But since the contours of the normative aspects of reality embrace the multifaceted nature of all cultures, their uniqueness and individuality can only be manifested within shared dimensions of normativity, for individuality and universality are not opposites, but mutually cohering traits of every concretely existing creature or societal reality.

The internal sphere of competence of every newly differentiated societal community and collectivity demands respect, but whenever this is not obtained, history tells the story of the many one-sided abuses of power, leading to situations where one sector of society violates the internal sphere-sovereignty of another. During the middle ages the Roman Catholic Church exceeded the limits of the church as an institution and excessively impinged upon the spheres of competence of the non-ecclesiastical domains of life. Likewise, after the Renaissance, the modern humanistic science ideal breached the integrity of every non-scholarly domain of life (Kant, in his *Critique of Pure Reason*, claimed that even law and religion cannot withdraw themselves from the critical scrutiny of reason).

What is excessive within historical development leads to disharmony within the process of cultural disclosure. In his extensive analysis of the historical process of disclosure (NC-II) Dooyeweerd specifies this point as follows:

> Any *excessive or extravagant* striving after power that ignores the fundamental modal principles of cultural economy and harmony, dashes itself to pieces against the power of the other differentiated cultural spheres. Or, if these have already lost the power to resist the usurper, it ends in the collapse of an entire culture. The history of the world offers many illustrations of this fundamental truth.

To this he adds that "without this cultural *eros* no single great work has come about in the course of the opened development of civilization. But this moment of *eros* in formative power can only disclose itself in a right way if the principles of cultural economy and harmony are respected. Otherwise cultural love is denatured to idolatry."

Finally Dooyeweerd shows how the aspect of faith guides the direction present in any cultural process of disclosure.

Disclosure can also take place within post-historical aspects, such as the jural aspect. Since the jural aspect is foundational to the moral (ethical) aspect, it may still only appear in its restrictive, "not yet disclosed," meaning. Such a system of penal law will still display all the constitutive meaning moments within the jural aspect. What is particularly striking in an undifferentiated society with an undisclosed jural awareness, is the dominance of a form of accountability on the basis of the *effects* of an action only (in German known as "Erfolgshaftung"). A person is held liable for the effects (consequences) of a deed without taking into account the *intentions* of the perpetrator – the well-known *lex talionis* applied the proportionality of an eye for an eye and a tooth for a tooth. On the one hand, this measure established a certain juridical balance, because one is not entitled to take a head for an eye. In undifferentiated societies, this configuration is intertwined with collective accountability.

Yet only when the jural awareness of a society and the juridical order of the state is regulatively deepened under the guidance of the aspect of moral love, will it be possible to account for the moral disposition of the perpetrator, for the subjective intentions of the person who committed the deed. Only then do the (disclosed) principles of jural morality come into play, such as the *fault* principle – in its two forms: *dolus* (intent) and *culpa* (culpability). In Dutch and German, the term 'Schuld' is normally translated as either fault or guilt. [Alan Cameron, who served as *Special Editor* of the *Introduction* of Dooyeweerd's *Encyclopedia of the Science of Law* points out that in English-speaking Common Law jurisdictions, "fault" is usually reserved for civil wrongs (torts) and "guilt" for criminal wrongs, but that Dooyeweerd "uses 'schuld' to refer to both types of wrong (i.e. to both civil and criminal delicts)." Therefore it can be translated as "fault" in a broader sense, not specific to any particular category of legal wrong.]

Contradiction and antinomy

The scope of the logical principles of identity and (non-)contradiction applies to the human ability to conceive and to argue. In his well-known *Introduction to Logic*, the logician, I.M. Copi states that the "principle of contradiction asserts that no statement can be both true and false" (1994 edition).

It was Immanuel Kant who provided us in his *Prolegomena* (1783) with the classical example of an illogical concept – namely that of a square circle. Establishing that this concept is illogical entails that a normative standard has been applied and that the said concept does not conform to the requirement of "ought to be" inherent in this normative standard. Confusing two spatial figures violates the demands for identifying and distinguishing properly: a square is a square (logically correct identification) and a square is not a non-square (such as a circle – logically correct distinguishing).

Thinking in a logically anti-normative way, i.e., thinking illogically, nonetheless remains bound to the structure of logicality and does not turn into something a-logical (non-logical), such as the economic, the moral or the jural. These (non-logical) facets of our experience are said to be a-logical but not illogical.

Consider now Zeno's paradox of the flying arrow. He states: "Something moving neither moves in the space which it occupies nor in the space it does not occupy" (B Fr.4). He commences by granting the reality of movement: "something moves," but then the troublesome question is asked: "Where does it move?" It neither moves in the space it occupies, nor in the space it does not occupy, therefore it after all does not move. What is granted initially, namely movement, is then frozen into distinct non-moving "moments" of time (static places in space). In the Volume dedicated to his theory of modal law-spheres (NC-II) Dooyeweerd points out that this antinomy results from the (theoretical) attempt to reduce movement (uniform flow) to static space. [An antinomy is literally a clash of laws. It confuses different modal aspects and is therefore inter-modal in nature. A logical contradiction, by contrast, confuses something within a modal aspect and in turn is intra-modal in nature – such as confusing two different spatial figures in the illogical concept of a square circle.

Such a conflict or clash between distinct functional (modal) laws indeed demonstrates the nature of a theoretical antinomy. After all, in the actual world these two modes of being are unique and are mutually cohering. Yet the attempt to reduce one unique mode to another invariably results in genuine (theoretical) antinomies.

In this sense antinomies therefore concern an inter-modal confusion, i.e., a lack of distinguishing properly between different modes, functions or aspects of reality.

Furthermore, an antinomy always entails a logical contradiction, whereas a contradiction does not necessarily presuppose an antinomy. The above-mentioned illogical concept of a "square circle" exemplifies an instance where two spatial figures are not properly identified and distinguished. In other words, a contradiction such as this has an intramodal character since its confusion relates to givens within the modal-functional boundaries of one aspect or function only. Zeno's attempt to reduce movement to space entails the contradiction: something moving can move if and only if it cannot move.

Historicism deifies the cultural-historical aspect for it not only claims that everything changes constantly, but that everything *is* history. However, only what is *not* intrinsically historical in nature, can *have* a history. Therefore it is precisely because the jural aspect, the economic aspect and the aesthetic aspect are not historical in nature that we can speak of *legal history*, *economic history* and *aesthetic history*. The irony of reductionist *ismic* modes of thinking is that they achieve the opposite of what is aimed for. If everything *is* history there is nothing left that can *have* a history.

We have noted that Dooyeweerd introduces a new ontic principle, the principle of the *excluded antinomy* (*principium exclusae antinomiae*). Since the principle of noncontradiction cannot establish which one of two contradictory statements is true, another principle is required to refer us beyond logic to the actual states of affairs needed within reality to decide which one is true. Leibniz discovered this principle and called it the *principium rationis sufficientis* (the principle of sufficient ground/reason). It is therefore the *excluded antinomy* which forbids inter-modal reductions (which invariably results in antinomies).

The Dimension of Ontic Time

ACCORDING TO DOOYEWEERD the dimension of time embraces all aspects and entities. What is unique and novel in his theory of time is that he does not reduce this dimension to one aspect only, such as physical time. He distinguishes between time on the law side of reality (time order) and time at the factual side (time duration). For example, the biotic time order for "the more highly developed organisms" is revealed in the succession of birth, growth, maturation, aging and dying – correlated with the widely differing life-spans of individual living entities.

In his work on the foundations of physics (1980) Stafleu relates time measurement to the first four modal aspects:

> This is most clearly shown by an analysis of the historical development of time measurement. Initially, time measurement was simply done by counting (days, months, years, etc.) Later on, time was measured by the relative position of the sun or the stars in the sky, with or without the help of instruments like the sundial. In still more advanced cultures, time was

measured by utilizing the regular motion of more or less complicated clockworks. Finally, in recent developments time is measured via irreversible processes, for example, in atomic clocks.

The phases through which time measurement developed, reflecting different modes of explanation, can be correlated with the *units of measurement* identified by Lorenzen in his *protophysics* (1976 and 1989). He distinguishes four units which reflect the four modes of explanation operative in the just-mentioned history of time measurement, namely *mass*, *length*, *duration* and *charge*. This shows that the generally accepted understanding of time (linking it merely with duration) is actually embedded in a context embracing diverse modes of explanation.

Heisenberg (1958), for example, accepts two universal constants (Einstein's postulate of the velocity of light and Planck's quantum of action). Yet he was looking for a third universal constant, namely a universal *length*. He claims that one has to have at least three units – be they *length*, *time* and *mass* or replaced by *length*, *velocity* and *mass* or even *length*, *velocity* and *energy*.

However, Dooyeweerd's analysis of the first four (irreducible) modal aspects of reality would have helped physicists to realize that *four units* are indeed needed. Clearly these four units of measurement reflect the meaning of the four foundational aspects of reality captured in the diagram below, namely *number* ('mass'), *space* ('length'), the *kinematic aspect* ('duration') and the *physical aspect* ('charge'). Weinert (1998) mentions even that usually physicists "distinguish fundamental constants from conventional units" – and he then lists the *kilogramme* (number), the *meter* (space), the *second* (the kinematic) and *temperature* (the physical).

	Lorenzen	Heisenberg (a)	Heisenberg (b)	Heisenberg (c)	Heisenberg (d)	Weinert
Physical	charge	quantum of action			energy	temperature
Kinematical	duration	c (velocity of light)	time	velocity	velocity	second
Space	length		length	length	length	meter
Number	mass		mass	mass		kilogram

It is clear that implicitly these thinkers account for different units of measurement in terms of the four most basic aspects of reality and it is also clear that they relate *time* rather to the *kinematic* aspect than exclusively to the physical mode.

Dooyeweerd's view entails that our awareness of time actually exceeds the confines of *physical time* (which is *homogenous*). The French-American biologist, Lecomte du Noüy, pointed out that the biotic phases of life are accelerating – birth, growth, maturation, aging and dying – thus showing that the life cycle of living entities is *heterogeneous* and therefore differs from physical time. Bergson introduced his understanding of *psychical duration*. Noteworthy is that

Hegel and Fichte introduced the concept of "geschichtliche Zeit" (historical time) – a theme that was followed up by Kierkegaard, Jaspers, Heidegger, and many others. In 1949 a Dutch professor in modern philosophy, discussed this new fashion in his inaugural lecture, "De Mensch als Historie" (*The historical nature of being human*) (Zuidema, 1949).

Dooyeweerd pointed out that all definitions of "time" are actually merely definitions of *diverse facets of time*. Against the fore-going background an alternative answer to this question will now be explored.

Do we live in a "space-time continuum"?

We are accustomed to mathematicians and physicists speaking of the *space-time continuum* in which we live. What they have in mind is Einstein's theory of relativity where time is added as fourth dimension to physical space. However, it is only mathematical space that is continuous, physical space is *not* continuous. The similarity between mathematical and physical space is that they are both *extended*, but within this similarity the difference is at once expressed: *spatial extension* is continuous in the sense that it allows for an infinite divisibility, whereas *physical space* is not continuous (since it is determined by the quantum-structure of energy) and is therefore not infinitely divisible. Almost a hundred years ago this difference was mentioned by David Hilbert (1925). In an article included in his *Abhandlungen zur Philosophie der Mathematik* (1976) Paul Bernays, the co-worker of Hilbert, also distinguishes between *physical space* and *mathematical space*: "Only through the contemporary development of geometry and physics did it become necessary to distinguish between space as something physical and space as an ideal multiplicity determined by spatial laws." Since concrete physical things are always quantized they cannot be divided *ad infinitum*. Of course one can revert to an aspectual mathematical *description* of processes involving energy (with reference to a *continuous variable*), but then the concreteness of physical entities is left behind while taking recourse to a *functional* mathematical notion – in which case it is indeed meaningful to hold that such a continuous variable entails infinite divisibility. Maddy (2005) implicitly alludes to this distinction: "But it is also true that the appearance of, say, a continuous manifold in our best description of space-time does not seem to be regarded as establishing the continuity of space-time; the micro-structure of space-time remains an open question."

So, strictly speaking, the popular conception of a space-time continuum is misplaced for it denies the difference between mathematical and physical space.

Time and the impasse of positivism

Positivism holds that the ultimate source of knowledge and truth is found in sensory perception. However, as soon as this maxim is tested with reference to *time* it turns out that an Achilles' heel of positivism is unmasked. Initially, in Greek culture, matter is described in *numerical* terms ("everything is number"), then in terms of *space* (the starting point of Greek space metaphysics and the medieval chain of being with God as *ipsum esse*), followed by employing *movement* as explanatory term (the classical mechanistic world view of the universe as *particles in motion*), and finally concluded with the acknowledgement of the characteristic *physical* nature of material things.

The key question is whether these aspectual terms could be observed in a sensory way. Can these terms be *weighed*, *touched*, *measured* or *smelled*? Just contemplate questions such as: What is the colour of the numerical aspect? What does the spatial aspect taste like? What does the kinematic aspect feel like? and What does the physical aspect sound like?

Likewise we may ask whether *time* can be observed by the senses – and if so, by which one(s)? Can we *touch* time? Can we *see* it? Can we *hear* it? Can we *smell* it? Every affirmative answer to these question will be absurd, showing that these *functional terms* as well as the term *time* cannot be observed by the senses. The reason is that neither time nor the various aspects of reality are concrete things. It is not difficult to realize that aspectual terms refer to a dimension of reality that is different from that of concrete (natural and societal) entities and processes. These entities and processes function within all the aspects of our experiential universe.

Consequently, the first step positivism had to take in order to digest "sense data" theoretically, has already eliminated the restriction of reliable knowledge merely to *sense data*!

That time cannot be identified with any single aspect also follows from these considerations. It is perfectly meaningful to speak of *temporal reality*, but it does not make sense to characterize reality exclusively in terms of a single aspect (such as the mentioned Pythagorean conviction that *everything is number*, the materialistic belief that *everything* is physical, the historicist claim that *all of reality is historical*, or the postmodern view that *everything is interpretation*). Dooyeweerd first developed his theory of modal aspects and entitary structures (designated as individuality structures), and only afterwards (probably in 1929) arrived at his first (radically new) understanding of what he called *cosmic time*. Traditional conceptions of time are constantly identifying time with merely one *aspect of time* – for example, as noted, when "true time" is seen as *physical*, *emotional duration* (Bergson), that it is *existential* in nature (where existence is understood in a *historical* sense – Heidegger), and so on.

The mere fact that we do speak of temporal reality rather suggests that time is a unique dimension of reality, cutting across the dimension of aspects and entities in its own way. Every attempt to define time invariably results in merely specifying one aspect of time – something repeatedly highlighted by Dooyeweerd in his seminal articles on time (which appeared in *Philosophia Reformata* in the late thirties of the 20th century): "Understandably traditional philosophy constantly attempted to delimit the time problem in a functionalistic manner. Time and again it identified universal cosmic time, which expresses itself at once in all modal aspects of reality because it provides the foundation for them all, with one of these modal aspects of time."

It is remarkable that the history of Western philosophy in many ways stumbled upon the *different modes of time* without being able to relate it to a general theory of *functional temporal modes*. Although Immanuel Kant believes that time is a form of (sensory) intuition, this psychological one-sidedness is transcended in his distinction between three 'modes' of time. His striking remark reads: "The three modes of time are endurance, succession and simultaneity" (CPR 1787).

Leibniz (1965), in turn, juxtaposes time – as "an order of successions," with space – as "an order of coexistences." Kant also realized that one has to distinguish between succession and causality – for although day and night succeed each other, it is meaningless to say that the day is the cause of the night or vice versa. In the 20th century, after modern physics was successful in transcending its mechanistic restriction, it was realized that physical time is intrinsically connected with causation, for the effect can never precede the cause. The numerical order of succession is *reversible* – manifested in the plus and minus directions of the system of integers, closed under the operations of addition, multiplication and subtraction. Saying that these operations are closed means that applying them to the set of integers always yield integers from the same set. When any two integers are added, multiplied or subtracted, the result is always another integer. The symmetry of any spatial configuration – allowing being turned upside down or front-backwards – shows the *reversibility* of the spatial time order, and the same applies to the kinematic time order, for the mathematical description of a constant movement (like the swinging of a pendulum) is equally valid in both directions (a mere switch of the sign provides a description in the opposite direction). Finally, the physical time order is *irreversible*.

Einstein (1959) explains the difference between physical irreversibility and kinematic (mechanical) reversibility:

> On the basis of the kinetic theory of gases Boltzman had discovered that, aside from a constant factor, entropy is equivalent to the logarithm of the 'probability' of the state under consideration. Through this insight he recognized the nature of courses of events which, in the sense of thermodynamics, are 'irreversible'. Seen from the molecular-mechanical point of view, however, all courses of events are reversible.

According to Janich (1975), the scope of an exact distinction between phoronomic (subsequently called kinematic by him) and dynamic arguments can be explained by means of an example. Modern physics has to employ a dynamic interpretation of the statement that a body can only alter its speed continuously. Given certain conditions, a body can never accelerate in a discontinuous way, that is to say, it cannot change its speed through an infinitely large acceleration, because this would require infinite force.

We have noted that the distinct manifestation of cosmic time within the first four modes is evident, particularly in the history of time measurement, where our general awareness of time concerns *earlier and later*, *simultaneity*, *time-flow* and *irreversibility* – all of them well-known *modalities of time*.

As soon as the meaning of (physical) change is analyzed, its dependence upon the three foundational modes of time is evident, because change presupposes (the modal meaning of) *constancy*, *simultaneity* and *succession*. In his work on space and time Grünbaum (1974) discusses Einstein's "principle of the constancy of the speed of light" and points out that it concerns an *upper limit* that is only realized in a *vacuum*.

Einstein's special theory of relativity proceeds from the hypothesis that one singular light signal has a constant velocity (in respect of all possible moving systems), without necessarily claiming that such a signal actually exists. Stafleu (1980) remarks: "The empirically established fact that the velocity of light satisfies the hypothesis is comparatively irrelevant."

Within the biotic aspect, as noted, the homogeneity of physical time is absent because the time phases correlated with the biotical time order are accelerated in the sense that the older a living entity gets, the quicker the process of aging occurs. Even the so-called "moment of death" eludes the scope of the physical understanding of time. Whatever criteria are used by the biologist, only once they have been applied and the living entity (plant, animal, or human being) is declared 'dead', the physicist may look at a physical clock and note the (thus externally correlated) "moment of death."

The sensitive mode adds its own unique modal meaning to the experience of time, for whereas it may feel as if a boring event takes hours, something intriguing or capturing one's attention may feel as if time passes very quickly. Pursuing an argument in a logical sense is only successful when conclusions are reached on the basis of *premises*. Even if the physical sequence of words mentions the conclusion before the premises, the logical time order (*prius et posterius*) will always be such that, in a logical sense, the *premises* precede the *conclusion*.

Similarly, within each of the post-logical aspects, the dimension of cosmic time "takes on" the original meaning of that specific aspect. Although the awareness of past, present and future rests upon a "more-than-modal-historical" reality, the demarcation of truly historical periods, eras and epochs is dependent on the functional time order within the cultural-historical aspect. Only when truly modal (and typical) historical criteria are applied, is it possible to understand the cultural meaning of historical eras. Such an assessment is always related to what are considered the historically significant events and tendencies that surfaced, and eventually became direction-giving and dominant within a particular era. If physical time was the only 'real' time, it would have been impossible to speak of peoples who are still living in the age of 'soft' cultures (predating the stone age) today, or about dwelling places of which one could say that there time "stood still."

The sign mode in turn reveals the meaning of cosmic time in its own way, for the temporal semantic effects of punctuation marks (or pausing in speech acts), are all relevant to what language users intend to convey. Likewise an awareness of social priorities is a reminder of social time – even in the case where one will allow an important person to go ahead in spite of one's own haste. Everyone will immediately understand that *interest* is intrinsic to economic time (not to forget the well-known expression: "time is money"). Within the aesthetic aspect, the dimension of cosmic time takes on a nuanced diversity of forms and shapes – depending upon the typical nature of different kinds and genres of art – such as the performing arts (bound to a limited duration and filling this time-span with a unique aesthetic expression), literature, and for example painting. But even in spite of the apparent timelessness of paintings and works of sculpture, they not only objectively last over time, but in an internal sense, also bring to expression their own aesthetic presence.

But perhaps hanging on to the "merely physical" nature of time receives its heaviest blow from the nature of jural time, for within this sphere, one sometimes encounters a different "calendar," recognizing no public holidays and Sundays in its contractual or legislative "count-down," and one also has to acknowledge laws with a *retroactive* effect. Through a declaration of age (*venia aetatis*) or as an effect of getting married, the jural time involved in "coming of age" may differ from the generally specified age of majority in the legal order of Western states.

Courtship and eventually getting engaged and married obey the normative time order of the moral aspect of love – although the duration of these successive events may vary considerably. Finally, within the certitudinal aspect, practically all religions distinguish an order of spiritual growth, correlated with a factual enrichment and maturation in faith. Through the eye of faith, the temporal is appreciated with a view to eternity.

Clearly *time* exceeds the boundaries of any aspect of reality because it resides within a distinct foundational dimension of the world, that Dooyeweerd has called *cosmic time*. [Perhaps it would be less confusing to speak of *ontic time*, since the term *cosmic* reminds us too strongly of what is merely physical in nature.] Owing to this dimension we are entitled to speak of *temporal reality*. However, this possibility implies that we should recognize that the dimensions of time and functional aspects are lying at the basis of the dimension of concrete (many-sided) entities. No single entity is exhausted by any one of its functions because it is embedded in the inter-modal and inter-structural temporality of reality embracing also the just-mentioned third dimension of reality. These three dimensions are indeed constitutive for our being-in-the-world, they form the experiential horizon of humankind.

It is only within the human selfhood, the human I-ness, that we transcend these three dimensions, because this radical and central depth dimension opens up the ultimate human awareness of and concern for *time-transcendent eternity*. Whether or not we are sharing this perspective is not a matter of rational argumentation, but one of ultimate commitment. Affirming the *temporality* of creation implicitly assumes the *eternity* of the Creator.

Augustine was right after all – when we do not reflect on time our intuitive (lived-through) experience of time is *integral*, *natural* and unproblematic, but as soon as we attempt to *conceptualize* time we find ourselves confronted by the baffling dispersion of the different ways in which we can distinguish modal aspects of time. Every time-concept, albeit that of the numerical time order of succession, the spatial awareness of simultaneity, the kinematic time order of uniform flow, and so on, presupposes the concept-transcending nature of cosmic time that lies at the foundation of all our time-concepts. The temporal existence (persistence in time) of every individual entity is not the mere sum of its modal functions since as such it belongs to another unique dimension of reality, distinct from but founded in those of *modal aspects* and *cosmic time*. This distinction prevents us from either falling prey to a "bundle-theory" or a "substance-theory" regarding the nature of many-sided concrete entities.

Since our *concepts of time* presuppose this integral and distinct dimension of *cosmic time* they are always, in a regulative sense, dependent upon our *idea of time* (i.e., our concept-transcending knowledge of time). What is indeed *baffling* about *cosmic time* is that it exceeds every possible concept of time we can obtain and therefore ultimately can only be approximated in a *concept-transcending idea*.

The Dimension of (Natural and Societal) Entities

Natural and societal entities, as well as all events (processes), in principle function in *all* the modal aspects or reality. Reminiscent of our brief indication of all the subject functions of a human being within all the aspects of reality, we may now apply the same method to reflect briefly on the functioning of the state within the various (ontic) modal functions of reality.

First of all, the state comprises a *multiplicity of individuals* normally designated as its *citizens*. Every *census* underscores this active function of the state within the quantitative aspect of reality. Keep in mind that this numerical function affirms one of the many modes of being of the state. Moreover, the existence of the state is certainly not exhausted by its numerical functioning. The most striking feature of the spatial function of a state is given in its *territory*. In spite of the fact that the citizens of a state are constantly *on the move*, i.e., interacting with other citizens, they remain bound to the state. In fact, one of the hallmarks of a democratic state is that it should provide for the freedom of movement of its subjects. In addition to the kinematic function, the state also functions within the physical aspect. By organizing the "power of the sword" the state is capable of exercising the required *force* whenever necessary – in service of restoring law and order when certain legal interests have been encroached upon (think about the actions of the police or the defense force). In popular parlance we are used to hear of *law-enforcement*. Undoubtedly the term *force* stems from the physical aspect of energy-operation and in this context, it clearly elucidates the function of the state within the physical aspect.

The state as a public legal institution binds together the *lives* of its citizens in specific ways. Tax-paying shows that every productive citizen indirectly dedicates some part of his or her time to the state. A certain portion of the life time of these citizens actually belongs to the state.

Furthermore, owing to the need to maintain its territorial integrity against possible threats from outside, a defense force is required, running the risk of citizens being *killed* in military action. Clearly, the life and death of citizens assume their own roles within the state as an institution – and it undeniably testifies to the fact that the state does function within the biotic aspect of reality as well. The state exhibits a biotic function in that its citizens are alive, reflected in the need to deal with public health and regulations regarding natural environmental. The nation of a state (transcending diverse ethnic communities without eliminating their right of continued existence), always operates on the basis of a national consciousness and an emotional sense of *belonging*. Although not all citizens may share this sentiment, a proper state should succeed in making its citizens *feel at home* (the notion of a *Heimat*). These phenomena clearly cannot be divorced from the *sensitive-psychic function* of the state. Furthermore, once we realize that citizens ought to feel at home within the state, they can also positively *identify* with it (compare the ID-documents of citizens). This function illustrates the political content of what sociologists call the 'we' and the 'they' – those belonging to this state and those not belonging to it. Since the core meaning of the logical-analytical aspect is captured in the reciprocity of *identification* and *distinguishing*, it is clear that whoever identifies something is also involved in distinguishing it from something else. The national identity of the citizens of the state testifies to the fact that this identity can't be understood only by recognizing the function of the state within the logical-analytical aspect (of identifying and distinguishing). Citizens are capable of rational interaction such that their functioning within the logical-analytical aspect of reality provides a basis for the *public opinion* within any particular state.

The cultural-historical aspect of reality concerns formations of *power*, since it brings to expression the basic trait of culture, namely the uniquely human calling to disclose the potential of creation in a process of cultural development. Such a process goes hand-in-hand with an ongoing development of human society in which – through increasing differentiation and integration of specific societal zones or spheres – distinct societal collectivities, including the state, in the course of time emerge. It is only on the basis of its "sword power" that the state can function as a *public legal institution*, since maintaining a public legal order depends on a monopoly of the "sword power" within the territory of the state. Of course the function of the state in the historical aspect is also seen in the actual history of every independent state. Then, that the state has a function within the sign mode of reality is obvious from its national symbols (anthem, flag, etc.) and from its official language(s). Similarly, the function of the state within the social aspect of reality is evident in the way in which it binds together its citizens within a public legal institution. It thus determines a specific kind of social interaction. Participating in a general election, acquiring an ID, observing traffic rules, respecting the rights of fellow citizens – and many more forms of social interaction, exemplify the function of the state within the social aspect of inter-human social intercourse.

Through taxes the state is enabled to fulfill its legal obligations in governing and administering a country, which brings to light an element of the economic function of the state. Given the significance of trade and commerce "political economy" focuses on the financial duties of a government. Although a state is not a work of art it does have the task of *harmonizing* clashing legal interests. Establishing balance and harmony amongst the multiplicity of legal interests within a differentiated society is always guided by the jural function of the state. In addition to this internal coherence between the jural and aesthetic aspects of the state the latter also has an external (i.e. original) function within the aesthetic aspect, displayed in the characteristic format of published (promulgated) state laws, in the aesthetic qualities of governmental buildings (houses of parliament, jails), and so on. The idea of public justice is not possible if the state does not actively function within the jural aspect of reality. The state also requires mutual respect between government of subjects as well as an ethical integrity amongst its citizens, for without this loyalty, the body politic will fall apart (of course the government must also conform to standards of public decency and integrity in order to avoid vices like nepotism and corruption). The nation of a state must share in its vision, its convictions regarding establishing a just public legal order through which each citizen receives its due. It is on this basis only that the highly responsible task of governing a country could be entrusted to its office-bearers. Terms like 'trust', 'certainty' and 'faith' are synonymous. The certitudinal or fiduciary aspect of reality – the faith aspect – is therefore not foreign to the existence of the state. Apart from party political differences mutual trust between government and subjects is an important ingredient of a stable state organization. And every political party operates on the basis of a specific political *confession of faith* (its *credo*).

The structural principle for being human embraces four distinct substructures, each maintaining its own sphere-sovereignty but at once also functioning within the enkaptic whole of the human body. [The term enkapsis designates forms of intertwinement where the internal spheres of operation of substructures are left intact. The Figure below is self-explanatory in this context.

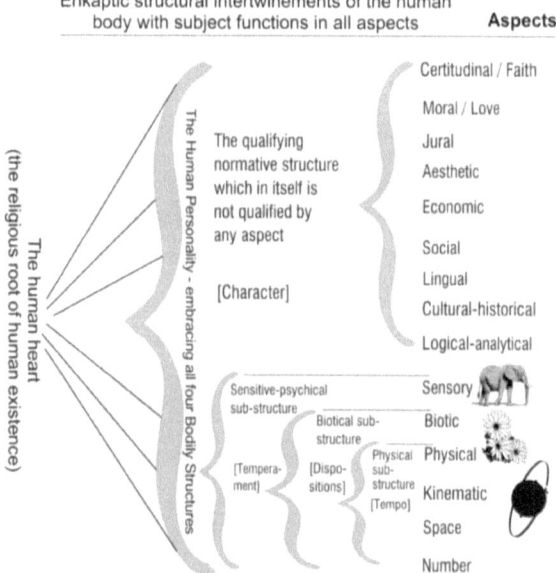

The Human Being - a Religious Personality

Enkaptic structural intertwinements of the human body with subject functions in all aspects   **Aspects**

The human heart (the religious root of human existence)

The Human Personality - embracing all four Bodily Structures

The qualifying normative structure which in itself is not qualified by any aspect

[Character]

- Certitudinal / Faith
- Moral / Love
- Jural
- Aesthetic
- Economic
- Social
- Lingual
- Cultural-historical
- Logical-analytical

Sensitive-psychical sub-structure — Sensory
Biotical sub-structure — Biotic
[Temperament] [Dispositions] Physical sub-structure — Physical
[Tempo] — Kinematic
Space
Number

The human heart, soul or spirit - understood in its radical, central and total sense - is the religious root of the human personality transcending its embodiment in the four enkaptically interwoven structures

Enkapsis concerns the interlacement of two differently-natured structures such that each retains its inner sphere of operation. The constitutive physical configuration of living things does not lose its physical-chemical qualification when it functions within living entities. Such entities are functioning enkaptically – that is, retaining their physically qualified nature – within living things. Similarly, the biotic organs and the sensory sub-structures of the human body are enkaptically interwoven in the total bodily existence of a person.

Undifferentiated societies

In the third Volume of his *A New Critique of Theoretical Thought* Dooyeweerd develops a penetrating analysis of the structure of undifferentiated societies by contrasting them with differentiated societies, within which each distinct social form of life has its own form of organization. The administration of the state differs from that of a business enterprise, a university, an ecclesiastical denomination, and so on. These distinct forms of organization are dependent upon one or another unique aspect of reality serving as its *characteristic* or *qualifying function* (*guiding function*). This means that the actions of a state, embracing government and subjects, are directed by jural considerations, focused on the integration of a multiplicity of legal interests into one public legal order. Similarly, a business enterprise finds its guiding principle in the economic aspect, a sport club in the social aspect, a church denomination in the aspect of faith, and so on.

Yet within undifferentiated societies such a distinct qualifying function is absent, because within them the leading role is assigned to one of the intertwined *societal entities*. Since one of the interlaced societal entities fulfill the leading role, such an undifferentiated society in its totality will act in *different societal capacities*. As a whole it will act as an *economic entity* which is equivalent to what we discern within a differentiated society as a business enterprise. The same applies to the whole of society acting as a *political unit*, which within differentiated societies will assume the form of a state. Because undifferentiated societies share in an undifferentiated organizational form, the possibility of any of the above-mentioned differentiated qualifying functions is absent. The variety of social forms of life which eventually, in the course of a gradual process of cultural-historical differentiation and disclosure, surface, are bound together in an undifferentiated manner within such an undifferentiated society. From this angle we can state that an undifferentiated society does not merely exhibit an economic aspect, because as a whole it acts as something which is recognized on a differentiated cultural level as an economically qualified business (whether it be of a hunting-, agricultural or cattle farmer type). An undifferentiated society also does not merely exhibit a juridical aspect, for it acts as a whole as something similar to what much later is identified as a *state* within a differentiated society. The same applies to the faith aspect – the undifferentiated society acts as a whole in a cultic-religious capacity, similar to a differentiated collective faith community. Within the undifferentiated total organizational form, a variety of typical structural branches are therefore found such that each one of them, alternatively, can bring into action the entire undifferentiated society. Within differentiated societies distinct and independent societal forms of life perform these activities.

In addition to the *Grossfamilie* (extended family) the *sib* also represents an undifferentiated society. The *sib* (as the Americans designate it) or the *clan* (as

British anthropologists prefer to denote it) is more encompassing, while the *tribe* displays a stronger (political) organization. This state of affairs implies that the correlate of an undifferentiated foundation (viz. one encompassing form of organization) is given in what may be called an *undifferentiated qualification*, because instead of a qualifying aspect of reality, one of the "not-yet-differentiated" societal structures, intertwined within the encompassing whole, assumes the leading or guiding role. In the case of the extended family, which binds parents, children and grandchildren together in a patriarchal unit, the patriarch and the oldest son are positioned in such a way that it reflects a specific kind of historical organization which cannot be explained exclusively on the basis of the blood relationship existing between them.

The extended family does not only evince a family structure, because in its undifferentiated total structure, other social forms of life are also intertwined. In particular the intertwined political structure is observed in the (political) force with which internal order and peace is maintained. Similarly the economic enterprise is recognized by the way in which the subsistence economy operates. However, the decisive question is: can we establish which one of the interwoven social forms of life present in such a society actually plays a leading role in its undifferentiated total structure? It appears that within the *Grossfamilie* the interwoven extended family structure is truly of a central leading nature even though as such it does not inherently possess an enduring structure of super- and sub-ordination.

The *sib* (clan or *gentes*), which apparently only appears when agriculture and livestock farming partly or completely replaces hunting as the basis of economic life, is constituted by a larger group of organized relations (where either only the father's or the mother's line of descent is taken into account). Although membership in the extended family is normally dependent upon blood relationship (natural birth), the sib is so large that it is no longer possible to assume direct descent from a communal father – although such descent may function as a fictitious presupposition or mythological conception. Besides activities like the ancestor cult (typical of an eventually differentiated cultic institution), taking revenge (which at a higher level of development is taken by an independent state), and the presence of forms of division of labour, also the family structure is present in the sib. In reality this interwoven family structure takes on the undifferentiated leading role within the sib – a leading role which, as noted above, rests on a particular historical form of power organization (just as in the case of the extended family). This feature anticipates the stronger political organization of the tribe.

Although tribal law ensured the presence of particular kinds of a legal order, there was still no uniform integration of legal rules, apart from the fact that every tribe had its own law.

As Roman folk law the *ius civile* right from its inception is reminiscent of the undifferentiated, tribal background of Roman life. However, during the expansion of the Roman Empire nonRomans were soon present on Roman territory. This situation increasingly called for some kind of a juridical arrangement in order to make legal provision for these non-Romans within the Roman Empire. This was done in what emerged as the *ius gentium*. Although this new legal development is sometimes seen as the starting point of what later became known as the *law of nations*, it should actually rather be seen as the starting point of civil private law and therefore not as the legal source of the law of nations. The subsequent legal development transcended the artificial intermediate position of *Latini* as a class between foreigners and Roman citizens.

During the feudal era guilds and manors continued the relatively undifferentiated sub-structure of medieval society, which the Church as the all-encompassing supra-natural institute of grace, destined to bring humankind to eternal bliss.

The state within a differentiated society

Because the guild system obstructed the realization of a genuine state-organization it was imperative for the differentiation of society to break down the artificial hold of power of the

Roman Catholic Church. This increasingly occurred during the period subsequent to the Renaissance, which witnessed a process of societal differentiation taking shape. This process was decisive for the emergence of the modern state because it generated the *distinct legal interests* which eventually had to be bound together within the public legal order of the state. The first major step in this process of differentiation is therefore given in dissolving the unified ecclesiastical culture of the Roman Catholic Church. This process initiated the differentiation of church and what eventually became known as the *state*. Also later on, in a similar process of differentiation, the nuclear family and the business enterprise gave shape to their own distinct sphere of operation during the industrial revolution.

At least one can partially see the disintegration of the unified ecclesiastical culture of the late medieval period as the outcome of the untenable synthesis between ancient Greek views and those of biblical Christianity.

A human person can assume a variety of social roles without ever being fully absorbed by any one of them.

From the perspective of the modern state the implication of this insight is that one can look at the citizens of a state from the perspective of any societal entity distinct from the state. For example, a particular group of citizens may be identified as Protestants, Catholics or Atheists. Changing the point of view may lift out just the married men or women within the territory of a state. Once again a subset of the citizens of a state may belong to one or another cultural (ethnic) community. In none of these instances will the angle of approach pursued in such an exercise coalesce with the *totality* of the citizens of the state, because the public legal character of the state distinguishes itself as cutting through all the non-public ties citizens may have. For this reason the societal collectivities that are distinct from the state have to integrate their own internal order-arrangements and these are always restricted to a specific sphere of private law. Therefore these social entities can only form *specific law*, a *ius specificum* which finds its counterpart in the *ius publicum* of the state.

The implication of these distinctions is that the only way to speak of the citizens of a state is precisely to *disregard* all the social ties citizens may have in diverse non-political societal entities. Asking whether or not a person is a citizen of a state is therefore disregarding a person's denominational stance, whether or not a person is married, studies or teaches at a particular university, is a member of a sport club, or has shares in one or another business enterprise.

Yet there is an important catch in speaking of *disregarding* the various non-state ties of citizens, because every one of those connections forms part of a societal entity with its own particular *legal interests*. Therefore, while disregarding these societal ties, the government of a modern constitutional state under the rule of law at the same time has to integrate these legal interests within its unified public legal order, while acknowledging that the internal spheres of operation of these non-political entities are not *generated* or *brought into being* by the state. The state can merely *acknowledge* these legal interests, with their accompanying limited (non-state) spheres of competence. If these spheres of competence would be derived from the state – and not merely acknowledged – then the state in fact would have been the all-encompassing totality of human society – which then would have been totalitarian and absolutist in the fullest sense of the word.

In various publications Dooyeweerd analyzed the influence of modern nominalism on the development of Western society. In no less than eighteen different places of his work, *The Struggle for a Christian Politics* (2012), Dooyeweerd highlights the influence of the ideas of Marisilius von Padua and Jean of Jandun. Particularly the idea of *popular sovereignty* surfaced prominently in their 1324 work on *In Defense of Peace* (*Defensor Pacis* – 1522). Dooyeweerd also dedicated a whole Treatise to "The Debate about the Concept of Sovereignty" (1950).

Subsequently it was Jean Bodin who introduced the concept of *sovereignty* in service of an understanding of the *authority* (power) of a government. In his work, *Six Books on the State* (Sechs Bücher über den Staat – 1576), he still designated a state as a *republic* while using the word *etat* for *specific forms* of the state. Unfortunately he did not succeed in liberating his thought from the traditional universalistic perspective that proclaims the state to be the *encompassing whole of society*. Where he portrays how families, corporations and colleges relate to the state, it is done in terms of the relationship between the *whole* (the state) and its parts. This encompassing view hampered his understanding of the process of differentiation because he observed in the legal competence of law-making societal entities, distinct from the state, a threat to the sovereignty of the state. Of course exactly the opposite is the case, for without the crystallization of distinct societal spheres each with their peculiar (non-political) legal interests, the state would not be able to integrate a diversity of legal interests into one public legal order. Whereas his idea of *sovereignty*, as characteristic feature of the government of a state, forms part of the significant process of differentiation taking shape after the Middle ages, Dooyeweerd points out that his un-grounded fear, that newly emerging spheres of legal competence would threaten the sovereign law-making competence of the state, stood in the way of positively appreciating societal differentiation. Next to the differentiation of church and state the industrial revolution accomplished the differentiation of the nuclear family and the modern business enterprise. It is therefore not surprising that the 19th century gave rise to the prominent modern democratic states, such as Germany, the Netherlands, France and Britain as well as Australia, New Zealand, the USA and Canada.

Unless an account is given of the *limited* sphere of competence of the state, no escape would be possible from a totalitarian view. The first element of this limitation concerns the *inner spheres of operation* of non-political societal entities and the second in acknowledging the necessity of an exclusive *legal domain* of the state, namely its *territory*.

When one abstracts from all societal communities and collectivities within which an individual may participate as a part of a larger whole, a personal sphere of freedom comes to light. As noted earlier, the expanding Roman Empire gave rise of the *ius gentium* which forms the point of departure of our modern *civil private law*. The latter allows the expression of personal freedom of thought, freedom of association, freedom of economic endeavours, of speech, of faith, and so on. As a coordinational sphere of law [Dutch: *maatschapsrecht*] civil private law lacks any relation of super- and sub-ordination. It concerns individuals (and societal entities) on equal footing, next to or in opposition to each other. In an article on *The Relationship between Individual and Community in the Roman and Germanic Conceptions of Property* (1962) Dooyeweerd characterizes *civil private law* as follows: "Civil law, according to its entire structure as a differentiated legal system, is the asylum of the individual person, the fortress for the protection of the individual person within legal life."

Both the state and civil private law are qualified by the *jural* aspect of reality. But civil private law cannot exist apart from the state and the non-political spheres of life. These non-political spheres of life fall within the domain of *non-civil private law*. Conversely, communal and collective spheres of law cannot exist apart from civil private law. The qualifying functions of the non-political spheres of life are different from the *jural* qualifying function of the state and of civil private law. Moreover, the constitution of modern states forms the originating source of diverse legal spheres of competence within a differentiated society (the last Volume of Dooyeweerd's *Encyclopaedia of the Science of Law* is dedicated to the theory of the *Sources of Law*). As a *formal* source of law the constitution of a modern democratic state contains stipulations regarding *materially different* spheres of law. Consider the domain of civil private law (common law and human rights), constitutional law (including the procedure according to which, through general elections, a government is put into office), and so on. The state is the only institution integrating a multiplicity of legal interests into *one public legal order* within its territory.

We are now in a position to explain what the idea of a *just state* (*Rechtsstaat*) according to Dooyeweerd entails.

> A just state presupposes multiple spheres of law within a differentiated society, including the domain of public law, civil private law and non-civil private law. The domain of public law embraces constitutional law, the law of nations, administrative law, penal law, and the law of criminal procedure. It guarantees and protects the political freedoms of citizens, such as the freedom to express political views, to organize political parties, to criticize the government, the right to protest, and the right to participate in the capstone of

political freedom, the right to vote (and to be elected). The domain of personal freedom (common law or civil private law) concerns the participation of individuals and societal entities on equal footing in the legal intercourse of a differentiated society. The domain of societal freedoms (non-civil private law) relates to the existence of non-political spheres of law that are co-constitutive for the existence of a just state (*Rechtsstaat*), for without them a substantial part of the legal interests to be protected by a government would be absent. On the basis of the monopoly over the sword power a *Rechtsstaat* has to harmonize and balance the multiplicity of legal interests on its territory and restore any infringement of rights in a retributive way.

When a differentiated society is characterized by the presence of political freedoms, personal freedoms (freedoms belonging to the domain of civil private law) and societal freedoms (the internal spheres of freedom of societal forms of life distinct from the state), the conditions for a just state are met. In other words, a just state (*Rechtsstaat*) is constituted by the spheres of public law, civil private law and non-civil private law with their accompanying freedoms.

THE DIMENSION OF ENTITIES | 105

Public law, civil private law and non-civil private law

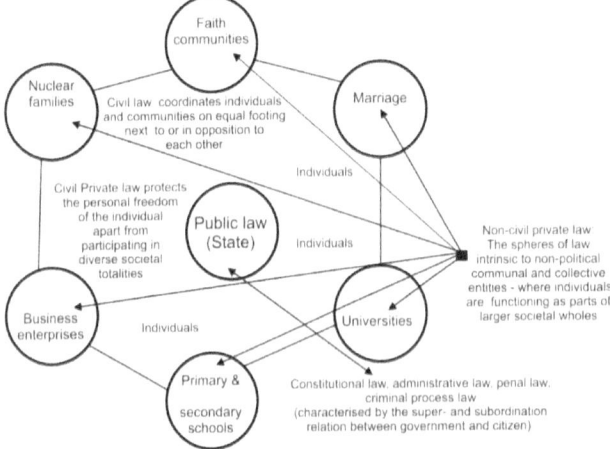

The Legacy of Reformational Philosophy

REFORMATIONAL PHILOSOPHY has adherents around the world. Since 1982 the *Foundation for Reformational Philosophy*, more or less every five years, have held International Conferences attended by 200 to 250 participants from more than 20 Countries worldwide. A number of scholars constructively employed Dooyeweerd's transcendental-empirical method within various academic disciplines. Normally this requires an account of the elementary basic concepts, the compound basic concepts and the typical concepts. In the field of physics we can mention Stafleu (1968, 1972, 1980, 1987, 1989, 1999, 2002, 2004; Strauss 2009a); regarding the foundations of mathematics various publications of Strauss could be mentioned (1991, 2002a, 2003, 2003a, Chapter 2 of 2005, 2005a; 2006, 2011, 2013, 2014). Since the thirties of the previous century the Dutch biologist, Harry Diemer, explored the significance of Dooyeweerd's philosophical distinctions for the discipline of biology (1963) and after his untimely death in 1945 it was continued by Duyvené De Wit (1965 – see also Strauss 2005a, 2009, and 2010). In the field of Sociology Dooyeweerd himself contributed substantially (Volume III 1997 – see also 1986). Strauss published a book (2006a) and multiple articles (2002, 2004, 2006c, 2007) within this field. Weideman published within the field of (applied) linguistics (2009, 2011 – see also Strauss 2008, 2013). Goudzwaard explored to economic sphere (1961, 1974, 1975, 1979). Apart from what Dooyeweerd developed in his *Encyclopedia of the Science of Law*, his successor Henk Hommes expanded his ground-breaking contribution significantly (1961, 1972, 1976, 1981, 1986). Chaplin (2011) and Koyzis (1993, 2003) contributed to the domain of political theory. In the field of theology Troost (2004, 2005, 2012) and Ouweneel should be mentioned (2014b – during the past decade the latter published an extensive 13 Volume *Dogmatics*). Of course this brief overview is not exhaustive, but simply a first indication of the wide range of disciplines within which scholarly work on the basis of Dooyeweerd's *Philosophy of the Cosmonomic Idea* has been done.

At half a dozen State Universities within the Netherlands the *Foundation* has established *Special Chairs in Reformational Philosophy* granting students the opportunity to study reformational philosophy while sponsoring appointed professors to teach this. Among the adherents of this philosophy, now already moving into its third generation, scholars from major natural sciences and humanities are found. The *Collected Works* of Dooyeweerd are in the process of being published. These will comprise 25 Volumes.

Works of Dooyeweerd have been translated into Japanese, Korean, Chinese, Spanish. Recently by Martin Jandl (2010) published a book in German: *Praxeologische Funkionalontologie, Eine Theorie des Wissens als Synthese von H. Dooyeweerd und R.B. Brandom*. [Jandl translated Roy Clouser's *Myth* (2005) into German: *Mythos der religiösen Neutralität* (2015).]

Selected List of Sources

Bernays, P. 1976. *Abhandlungen zur Philosophie der Mathematik*. Darmstadt: Wissenschaftliche Buchgesellschaft.

Bodin, J. 1981. *Sechs Bücher über den Staat*, Buch I-III. Übersetzt und mit Anmerkungen versehen von Bernd Wimmer, Eingeleitet und herausgegeben von P.C. Meyer-Tasch. München: Verlag C.H. Beck.

Botha, M.E. 2006. Metaphor, embodiment and fiduciary beliefs in science. (In: Lategan, L.O.K. & Smith, J.H. *Time and context relevant philosophy*. Festschrift dedicated to D.F.M. Strauss. Bloemfontein: Association for Christian Higher Education. p. 17-36.)

Botha, M.E. 2007. *Metaphor and its moorings, studies in the grounding of metaphorical meaning*. Bern: Peter Lang.

Cameron, A.M. 2000. Implications of Dooyeweerd's Encyclopedia of Legal Science. In: Dooyeweerd 200:191-238.

Chaplin, J. 2011. Herman Dooyeweerd, Christian Philosopher of State and Civil Society. Notre Dame: University of Notre Dame Press.

Clouser, R. 2015. *Mythos der religiösen Neutralität*. Übersetzer, Martin Jandl. Leiden: E.J. Brill.

Clouser, R.A. 2005. *The Myth of Religious Neutrality: An Essay on the Hidden Role of Religious Belief in Theories*. Notre Dame: University of Notre Dame Press (new revised edition, first edition 1991).

De Wit Duyvené, J.J. 1965. The impact of Herman Dooyeweerd's Christian Philosophy upon Present day Biological thought, In: *Christianity and Philosophy*, Philosophical Essays dedicated to Dr. Herman Dooyeweerd. Kampen: Kok (pp.405-433).

Diemer, J.H. 1963. *Natuur en Wonder*. Christelijke Perspectief Vol. VI, (Red. J. Stellingwerf), Amsterdam: Buijten & Schippereijn.

Dooyeweerd, H. 1926. *De Beteekenis der Wetsidee voor Rechtswetenschap en Rechtsphilosophie* (The Significance of the Cosmonomic Idea for the Science of Law and Legal Philosophy), Inaugural Lecture Free University. Amsterdam October 15.

Dooyeweerd, H. 1928. Het juridisch causaliteitsprobleem in 't licht der Wetsidee. In. *Antirevolutionaire Staatkunde*. 1928(1):21-121.

Dooyeweerd, H. 1930. De Structuur der Rechtsbeginselen en de Methode der Rechtswetenschap in het Licht der Wetsidee (The Structure of legal principles and the method of the science of law in the light of the Cosmonomic Idea). In: *Wetenschappelijke Bijdragen, Aangeboden door Hoogleraren der Vrije Universiteit ter Gelegenheid van haar Vijgtigjarig Bestaan*. Amsterdam: De Standaard (pp.225-266).

Dooyeweerd, H. 1931. *Crisis in de Humanistsche Staatsleer.* Amsterdam: N.V. Boekhandel W. Ten Have.

Dooyeweerd, H. 1932. Norm en Feit, In: *Themis*, 93(E), pp.155-214.

Dooyeweerd, H. 1935-1936. *De Wijsbegeerte der Wetsidee.* 3 Vols. Amsterdam: Paris.

Dooyewerd, H. 1936. The Problem of Time and its Antinomies on the Immanence Standpoint I, *Philosophia Reformata*, Year 1, 2nd Quarter, pp.65-83.

Dooyewerd, H. 1939. The Problem of Time and its Antinomies on the Immanence Standpoint II, *Philosophia Reformata*, Year 4, 1st Quarter, pp.1-28.

Dooyewerd, H. 1940. The Problem of Time in the Philosophy of the Cosmonomic Idea I, *Philosophia Reformata*, Year 5, 3rd Quarter, pp.160-192.

Dooyewerd, H. 1940a. The Problem of Time in the Philosophy of the Cosmonomic Idea I, *Philosophia Reformata*, Year 5, 4th Quarter, pp.193-234.

Dooyeweerd, H. 1941. De transcendentale critiek van het wijsgeerig denken en de grondslagen van de wijsgeerige denkgemeenschap van het avondland. In: *Philosophia Reformata.* 6:1-20.

Dooyeweerd, H. 1948. *Transcendental Problems of Philosophic Thought.* Grand Rapids: WM. B. Eerdmans Publishing Company.

Dooyeweerd, H. 1949. *Reformatie en Scholastiek in de Wijsbegeerte*, Volume I, Het Griekshe Voorspel. Franeker: T. Wever.

Dooyeweerd, H. 1950. *De Strijd om het Souvereiniteitsbegrip in de moderne Rechts- en Staaatsleer.* Amsterdam: Paris.

Dooyeweerd, H. 1958. *Encyclopaedie der Rechtswetenschap.* Part I, Amsterdam: Bureau Studenteraad.[The date 1958 indicates the year in which Judge G.F. de Vos Hugo received his copy. It is identical to the copy that I have purchased in 1970 at the Free University of Amsterdam (available since 1967). It is also identical to an early sixties Volume sent to my father by Dooyeweerd (my father studied with Dooyeweerd in the thirties).]

Dooyeweerd, H. 1959. Schepping en Evolutie. In: *Philosophica Reformata,* 24:113-159.

Dooyeweerd, H. 1960. Van Peursen's Critische Vragen bij "A New Critique of Theoretical Thought." *Philosophia Reformata,* 25(3&4):97-150.

Dooyeweerd, H. 1962. Individu, Gemeenschap en Eigendom: In: *Verkenningen in de Wijsbegeerte, de Sociologie en de Rechtsgeschiedenis.* Amsterdam: Buijten & Schipperheijn (pp. 149-215).

Dooyeweerd, H. 1967 (to be published): *The Encyclopedia of the Science of Law,* Collected Works of Herman Dooyeweerd, A Series Vol. 9, General Editor D.F.M. Strauss; Special Editor Alan Cameron [The Dutch texts comprise (a) The Introduction, (b) The Historical Volume, (c) The Systematic Volume, (d) The Distinction between Public Law and Private Law and (e) The Theory of the Sources of Positive Law. References to the Dutch text will be to 1967-I (historical part) and 1967-II (systematic part).] Grand Rapids: Paideia Press.

Dooyeweerd, H. 1986. A Christian Theory of Social Institutions. Tr. Magnus Verbrugge, Introduction by John Witte, Jr., La Jolla: The Herman Dooyeweerd Foundation.

Dooyeweerd, H. 1996. *Christian Philosophy and the Meaning of History*, Collected Works, B Series, Volume 1, General Editor D.F.M. Strauss. Lewiston: Edwin Mellen.

Dooyeweerd, H. 1997. *A New Critique of Theoretical Thought*, Collected Works of Herman Dooyeweerd, A Series Vols. I-IV, General Editor D.F.M. Strauss. Lewiston: Edwin Mellen. Hay traducción al español: Una nueva crítica del pensamiento teórico, Volumen I, 2020, Jordan Station: Paideia Press.

Dooyeweerd, H. 1997a. Essays in Legal, Social and Political Philosophy. Collected Works of Herman Dooyeweerd, B Series Volume 2, General Editor D.F.M. Strauss, Lewiston: Edwin Mellen.

Dooyeweerd, H. 1999. In the Twilight of Western Thought. Collected Works of Herman Dooyeweerd, B Series, Volume 4, General Editor D.F.M. Strauss, Special Editor J.K.A. Smith. Lewiston: Edwin Mellen. Hay traducción al español: En el ocaso del pensamiento occidental, en prensa, Jorfdan Station: Paideia Press.

Dooyeweerd, H. 2000. Contemporary Reflections on the Philosophy of Herman Dooyeweerd, Collected Works of Dooyeweerd, Series C – Dooyeweerd's Living Legacy, Edited by D.F.M. Strauss and Michelle Botting. Lewiston: Edwin Mellen.

Dooyeweerd, H. 2004. *Political Philosophy*. D Series, Volume 1, General Editor D.F.M. Strauss. Lewiston: Edwin Mellen.

Dooyeweerd, H. 2008. *The Struggle for a Christian Politics*, B Series, Volume 5, General Editor D.F.M. Strauss, Lewiston: Edwin Mellen.

Dooyeweerd, H. 2012. *Encyclopedia of the Science of Law*, Series A, Volume 8/1, General Editor D.F.M. Strauss, Special Editor A.C. Cameron, Paideia Press: Grand Rapids.

Dooyeweerd, H. 2012. *Reformation and Scholasticism in Philosophy*, Vol.I, Collected Works of Herman Dooyeweerd, Series A, Volume 5, General Editor D.F.M. Strauss. Grand Rapids: Paideia Press.

Dooyeweerd, H. 2012a. *Roots of Western Culture, Pagan, Secular and Christian Options*, Series B, Volume 15, General Editor D.F.M. Strauss. Grand Rapids: Paideia Press. Hay traducción al español: Raíces de la cultura occidental, 2020, Barcelona: Editorial Clié.

Fichter, J.H. (comp. Erich Bodzenta) 1968. *Grundbegriffe der Soziologie*. Berlin: Springer Verlag.

Fourie, F.C.v.N. 1993. In the Beginning there Were Markets? (pp.41-65). In: *Transactions, Costs, Markets and Hierarchies*. Edited by Christos Pitelis. Oxford: Basil Blackwell.

Gadamer, H-G. 1989. *Truth and Method*, Second Revised Edition (first translated edition 1975). New York: The Continuum Publishing Company.

Goudzwaard, B. 1961. De economische theorie en de normatieve aspecten der werkelijkheid [Economic Theory and the Normative Aspects of Reality], *Perspectief*. Kampen: Kok, 1961:310-323.

Goudzwaard, B. 1974. *Schaduwen van het groei-geloof*. Kampen: Kok.

Goudzwaard, B. 1975. *Aid for the overdeveloped West*. Toronto: Wedge publishing foundation.

Goudzwaard, B. 1979. *Capitalism and progress: a diagnosis of Western society*; translated and edited by Josina Van Nuis Zylstra. Grand Rapids,Mich: Eerdmans.

Grünbaum, A. 1974. *Philosophical Problems of Space and Time*. Dordrecht (Holland): D. Reidel (second, enlarged edition).

Heisenberg, W. 1958. *Physics and Philosophy. The Revolution in Modern Science*. New York: Harper Torchbooks.

Hilbert D 1913. Über den Zahlbegriff. "Jahresbericht der Deutschen Mathematiker-Vereinigung," Reprinted in Hilbert D (1913), *Grundlagen der Geometrie*. Fourth revised and expanded edition (first edition 1899). Leipzig: Teubner BG, pp 237–242.

Hilbert, D. 1925. Über das Unendliche, *Mathematische Annalen*, Vol.95, 1925: 161-190.

Hilbert, D. 1970. *Gesammelte Abhandlungen*, Vol.3, Second Edition, Berlin: Verlag Springer.

Hommes, H. Van Eikema 1982. *Inleiding tot de wijsbegeerte van Herman Dooyeweerd*. The Hague: Martinus Nijhoff.

Hommes, H.J. 1961. *Een Nieuwe Herleving van het Natuurrecht*, Zwolle: W.E.J. Tjeenk Willink.

Hommes, H.J. 1972. *De Elementaire Grondbegerippen der Rechtswetenschap*. Deventer: Kluwer.

Hommes, H.J. 1976. *De Samengestelde Grondbgerippen der Rechtswetenschap*, Deventer: Kluwer.

Hommes, H.J. 1981. *Hoofdlijnen van de Geschiedenis der Rechtsfilosofie*, Deventer: Kluwer.

Hommes, H.J. 1986. *De Wijsgerige Grondslagen van de Rechtssociologie*. Deventer: Kluwer.

Janich, P. 1975. Tragheitsgesetz und Inertialsysteem. In: Frege und die moderne Grundlagenforschung, red. Chr. Thiel, Meisenheim am Glan: Hain.

Jandl, M. 2010. *Praxeologische Funkionalontologie, Eine Theorie des Wissens als Synthese von H. Dooyeweerd und R.B. Brandom.* Frankfurt am Main: Pete Lang.

Kalsbeek, L. 1970. *De Wijsbegeerte der Wetsidee, Proeve van een Christelijke filosofie.* Amsterdam: Buijten & Schipperheijn.

Kant, I. 1781. *Kritik der reinen Vernunft*, 1st Edition (references to CPR A). Hamburg: Felix Meiner edition (1956).

Kant, I. 1783. *Prolegomena zu einer jeden künftigen Metaphysik die als Wissenschaft wird auftreten können.* Hamburg: Felix Meiner edition (1969).

Kant, I. 1787. *Kritik der reinen Vernunft*, 2nd Edition (references to CPR B). Hamburg: Felix Meiner edition (1956).

Koyzis, D.T. 1993. Imaging God and His Kingdom: Eastern Orthodoxy's Iconic Political Ethic, *The Review of Politics*, 55(2):267-290. University of Notre Dame 1993 DOI: http://dx.doi.org/10.1017/S0034670500017381 (About DOI), Published online: 05 August 2009.

Koyzis, D.T. 2003. *Political Visions&Illusions. A Survey&Christian Critique of Contemporary Ideologies*. Downers Grove, Illinois: Intervarsity Press.

Koyzis, D.T. 2004. Introductory Essay, in Daniël F. M. Strauss, comp., Political Philosophy by Herman Dooyeweerd (Ancaster, Ontario and Lewiston, New York: The Dooyeweerd Centre and the Edwin Mellen Press, 2004), pp. 1-16, The Collected Works of Herman Dooyeweerd, series D, volume 1.

Leibniz, G.W.H. 1965. Correspondence with Clarke, Third Paper, published in the translation of M. Morris: *Leibniz, Philosophical Writings*, London: Everyman's Library.

Locke, J. 1966. *Two Treatises of Civil Government*. London: Everyman's Library (1690).

Lorenzen, P. 1976. Zur Definition der vier fundamentalen Meßgrößen. In: *Philosophia Naturalis*, Volume 16:1-9.

Lorenzen, P. 1976. Zur Definition der vier fundamentalen Meßgrößen. In: *Philosophia Naturalis*, Volume 16 (pp.1-9).

Lorenzen, P. 1989. Geometry as the Measure-Theoretic A Priori of Physics, in: Butts and Brown (Comps.), 1989:127-144.

MacIver, R.M. 1942. *Social Causation*, New York: Harper & Row (1964).

Maddy, P. 2005. Three forms of naturalism. In: Shapiro, 2005:437-459.

McIntire, C.T. (comp.) 1985. *The Legacy of Herman Dooyeweerd*. Lanham: University Press of America.

Ouweneel, W.J. 2014. *Wisdom for Thinkers, An Introduction to Christian Philosophy*. Grand Rapids: Paideia Press.

Ouweneel, W.J. 2014a. *Power in Service. An Introduction to Christian Political thought*. Grand Rapids: Paideia Press.

Ouweneel, W.J. 2014b. *What then is Theology? An Introduction to Christian Theology*. Grand Rapids: Paideia Press.

Ouweneel, W. J. 2014c. *Searching The Soul: An Introduction To Christian Psychology*. Grand Rapids: Paideia Press.

Popper, K. 1966. *The Open Society and its Enemies*, Vols. I & II, London: Routledge & Kegan Paul.

Russell, B. 1956. *The Principles of Mathematics*. London: George Allen & Unwin. (First published in 1903, Second edition 1937, Seventh edition 1956).

Seerveld, C.G. (Comps. John Kraay and Anthony Tol) 1979. Modal Aesthetics: Preliminary Questions with and Opening Hypothesis. In: *Hearing and Doing, Philosophical Essays Dedicated to H. Evan Runner*, Toronto: Wedge Publishing Foundation (pp.263-294).

Seerveld, C.G. .1987. Imaginativity. In: *Faith and Philosophy*, Vol.4, Nr.1, January.

Seerveld, C.G. .2001. Christian aesthetic bread for the world. In: *Philosophia Reformata*. 66(2):155-177.

Seerveld, C.G. 1958. Benedetto Croce's Earlier Aesthetic Theories and Literary Criticism. Kampen: J.H. Kok N.V.

Seerveld, C.G. 1968. A Christian Critique of Art and Literature. Toronto: The Association for Reformed Scientific Studies.

Seerveld, C.G. 1970. A Christian Tin-Can Theory of Man. In: *Journal of the American Scientific Affiliation*, Minnesota, August.

Seerveld, C.G. 1980. *Rainbows for the Fallen World: Aesthetic Life and Aesthetic Task*, Toronto.

Seerveld, C.G. 1985: Dooyeweerd's Legacy for Aesthetics: Modal Law Theory. In: McIntire, C.T. (comp.) 1985 (pp.41-79).

Shapiro, S. 2005 (Editor). *The Oxford Handbook of Philosophy of Mathematics and Logic*. Oxford: Oxford University Press.

Spier, J.M. 1972. *Oriëntering in die Christelike Wysbegeerte*, vertaal deur H.J. en D.F.M. Strauss. Bloemfontein: Sacum Beperk.

Stafleu, M.D. 2004. On the character of social communities, the state and the public domain. In: *Philosophia Reformata*. 69(2):125-139.

Stafleu, M.D. 1968. Individualiteit in de fysica. In: *Reflexies, Opstellen aangeboden aan Prof. Dr. J.P.A. Mekkes*. Amsterdam: Buijten & Schipperheijn.

Stafleu, M.D. 1972. Metric and Measurement in Physics. In: *Philosophia Reformata*, 37(1/2): 42-57.

Stafleu, M.D. 1980. *Time and Again, A Systematic Analysis of the Foundations of Physics*. Toronto: Wedge.

Stafleu, M.D. 1987. Theories at Work: On the Structure and Functioning of Theories in Science, in Particular during the Copernican Revolution, Lanham: University Press of America.

Stafleu, M.D. 1989. *De Verborgen Structuur*. Amsterdam: Buijten & Schipperheijn.

Stafleu, M.D. 1999. The idea of a natual law. In: *Philosophia Reformata*, 64 (1): 88-104.

Stafleu, M.D. 2002. *Een Wereld vol Relaties*. Amsterdam: Buijten & Schipperheijn.

Stegmüller, W. 1969. *Metaphysik, Skepsis, Wissenschaft*, (first edition 1954). Berlin/New York: Springer.

Strauss, D.F.M. 2008. The "Basic Structure of Society" in the Political Philosophy of John Rawls. In: *Politeia*, 27(1):28-46.

Strauss, D.F.M. 1973. *Begrip en Idee*. Assen: Van Gorcum.

Strauss, D.F.M. 1980. *Inleiding tot die Kosmologie*, Bloemfontein: VCHO.

Strauss, D.F.M. 1982. The Place and Meaning of Kant's Critique of Pure Reason (1781) in the legacy of Western philosophy. In: *South African Journal of Philosophy*, Volume 1, (pp.131-147).

Strauss, D.F.M. 1983a. Individuality and Universality. In: *Reformational Forum*, 1(1):23-36.

Strauss, D.F.M. 1984. An analysis of the structure of analysis, (The Gegenstand-relation in discussion). In: *Philosophia Reformata*. 49(1): 35-56.

Strauss, D.F.M. 1991. The Ontological Status of the principle of the excluded middle. In: *Philosophia Mathematica* II, 6(1):73-90.

Strauss, D.F.M. 2000. Kant and modern physics. The synthetic a priori and the distinction between modal function and entity. In: *South African Journal of Philosophy* (pp.26-40).

Strauss, D.F.M. 2001. *Paradigms in Mathematics, Physics, and Biology – their Philosophical Roots*. Bloemfontein: Tekskor (Revised Edition, 2004).

Strauss, D.F.M. 2001. Reductionism in Mathematics: Philosophical Reflections, in: *Journal for Christian Scholarship* (JCS), 37(1&2):1-14.

Strauss, D.F.M. 2002. The scope and limitations of Von Bertalanffy's systems theory. In: *South African Journal of Philosophy*, Volume 21, (pp.163-179).

Strauss, D.F.M. 2002. Is it meaningful to juxtapose "individual" and "society"? *Society in Transition*. 33(1):96-115.

Strauss, D.F.M. 2002a. Philosophical Reflections on continuity. In: *Acta Academica*, 34(3) (pp.1-32).

Strauss, D.F.M. 2003a. Frege's Attack on 'Abstraction' and his Defense of the 'Applicability' of Arithmetic (as Part of Logic). In: *South African Journal of Philosophy*, Volume 22, (pp.63-80).

Strauss, D.F.M. 2003b. Popper and the Achilles heel of positivism. In: Koers, Vol.68, Nr. 2 & 3(pp.255-278).

Strauss, D.F.M 2003d. Is a Christian Mathematics possible? *Journal for Christian Scholarship*, 2003(3&4):31-49.

Strauss, D.F.M. 2004. Transcending the impasse of individualism and universalism in sociological theory, *Society in Transition*. 35(1):165-182.

Strauss, D.F.M. 2005. Accounting for Primitive Terms in Mathematics, in: *Koers*, 70(3):515-534.

Strauss, D.F.M. 2005a. *Paradigmen in Mathematik, Physik und Biologie und ihre philosophische Wurzeln*. Frankfurt am Main: Peter Lang.

Strauss, D.F.M. 2006. The Concept of Number: Multiplicity and Succession between Cardinality and Ordinality, *South African Journal for Philosophy*, 25(1):27-47.

Strauss, D.F.M. 2006a. *Reintegrating Social Theory – Reflecting upon human society and the discipline of sociology*. Frankfurt am Main: Peter Lang.

Strauss, D.F.M. 2006b. The mixed legacy underlying Rawls's Theory of Justice, In: *Journal for Juridical Science*, 31(1):61-79.

Strauss, D.F.M. 2006c. Beyond the opposition of individual and society, Part I, Acknowledging the constitutive social function of being an individual and 'de-totalizing' the idea of 'society', *South African Review of Sociology*, December 2006, Vol.37, No.2:143-164.

Strauss, D.F.M. 2007. Beyond the opposition of individual and society, Part II, The 'category-mistake' entailed in this opposition, *South African Review of Sociology* 2007 Vol.38 No.1:1-19.

Strauss, D.F.M. 2007a. Did Darwin develop a theory of evolution in the biological sense of the word? In: *South African Journal of Philosophy*, Vol.26(2):190-203.

Strauss, D.F.M. 2008. The "modal grid" underlying Language, Communication, Translation and the Learning of a New

Language *Communitas*, Volume 13:2008: 117-34.

Strauss, D.F.M. 2009. *Philosophy: the Discipline of the Disciplines*. Grand Rapids: Paideia Press.

Strauss, D.F.M. 2009a. The Significance of a Non-Reductionist Ontology for The Discipline of Mathematics: A Historical and Systematic Analysis. *Axiomathes*: An International Journal in Ontology and Cognitive Systems (Springer Verlag, Berlin), 20:19-52.

Strauss, D.F.M. 2009b. The Significance of a Non-Reductionist Ontology for the Discipline of Physics: A Historical and Systematic Analysis. *Axiomathes*: An International Journal in Ontology and Cognitive Systems (Springer Verlag, Berlin), 20:53-80.

Strauss, D.F.M. 2009c. Dooyeweerd, Derrida and Habermas on the "force of law". In: South African Journal of Philosophy SAJP 28(1):65-87.

Strauss, D.F.M. 2010. A perspective on (neo-)Darwinism. Koers 74(3):341-386.

Strauss, D.F.M. 2011. Wysgerige Perspektiewe op Getal. *Lit*NET, On-line: http://www.litnet.co.za/Article/wysgerige-perspektiewe-op-die-uniekheid-van-getal.

Strauss, D.F.M. 2012. A history of attempts to delimit (state) law. In: *Journal for Juridical Science*, 37(2):35-64.

Strauss, D.F.M. 2012a. The paradigm of Weideman: Appreciating the uniqueness of language and scholarly disciplines. *Journal for Language Teaching* 46/2:172-189.

Strauss, D.F.M. 2013. Sphere Sovereignty, Solidarity and Subsidiarity. In: *Journal for Christian Scholarship*, 49(3):93-123.

Strauss, D.F.M. 2013a. World view, philosophy, and the teaching of arithmetic. *Acta Academica* 45(1): 26-57.

Strauss, D.F.M. 2014. What is a Line? In: *Axiomathes*: An International Journal in Ontology and Cognitive Systems (Springer Verlag, Berlin) (2014) 24:181–205; DOI 10.1007/s10516-013-9224-5.

Strauss, D.F.M. 2014a. The place of the state in a differentiated society: historical and systematic perspectives. In: *Politikon* 41(1):1-19.

Strauss, D.F.M. 2014b. The genesis of a new conception of the state in the legal and political philosophy of Dooyeweerd, In: JCS, 50(1&2):75-99.

Strauss, D.F.M. and Botting, M. (Comps.) 2000. Contemporary Reflections on the Philosophy of Herman Dooyeweerd. Lewiston: The Edwin Mellen Press.

Strauss, H.J. 1965. Nie-Staatlike Owerheidstaak in Beskawingsamehang. Philosophia Reformata. 30(2-4):198-204.

Troost, A. 2004. *Vakfilosofie van de Geloofswetenschap. Prolegomena van de Theologie*. Budel: Damon.

Troost, A. 2005. *Antropocentrische Totaliteitswetenschap. Inleiding in de 'reformatorische wijsbegeerte'*. Budel: Damon.

Troost, A. 2012. *What is Reformational Philosophy? An Introduction to the Cosmonomic Philosophy of Herman Dooyeweerd*. Grand Rapids: Paideia Press.

Van Peursen, 1995: Dooyeweerd en de wetenschapsfilosofische discussie, in: *Dooyeweerd herdacht*, edited by J. De Bruin, Amsterdam: VU-Uitgeverij.

Van Riessen, H. 1959. *Op Wijsgeerige Wegen*. Wagegingen: Zomer & Keuring (second edition 1963).

Van Riessen, H. 1970. *Wijsbegeerte*. Kampen: Kok.

Von Padua, M. 1522. *Defensor Pacis*. New Edition 1928. Cambridge: Prévité-Orton.

Weideman, A. 2009. *Beyond Expression. A systematic study of the foundations linguistics*. Grand Rapids: Paideia.

Weideman, A. 2011. *A Framework for the study of linguistics*. Grand Rapids: Paideia and Pretoria: Van Schaik.

Weinert, F. 1998. Fundamental Physical Constants, Null Experiments and the Duhem-Quine Thesis. In: *Philosophia Naturalis*, 35:225-251.

Weyl, H. 1946. Mathematics and Logic. In: *American Mathematical Monthly*, Vol. 53.

Wolters, A. 1981. Facing the Perplexing History of Philosophy. In: *Journal for Christian Scholarship*, 17(4):1-31.

Wolters, A. 2005. *Creation Regained, Biblical Basics for a Reformational Worldview*. Grand Rapids: Eerdmans.

Zuidema, S. U. 1948. *De Mensch als Historie*. Franeker: Wever.

INDICES

Name Index

A

Achilles	75
Adorno, T.	37
Amsterdam	5, 6, 13
Anaxagoras	20
Anaximander	19
Aquinas, Thomas	7, 24, 26
Aristotle	19, 21, 26, 45
Atheists	98
Augustine	7, 23, 84
Australia	101
Ayer, A.J.	37

B

Baden school	36
Bergson, H.	73, 77
Berkeley, G.	29
Bernays, Paul	74
Bible	23
Bloch, E.	37

Bodin, Jean	100
Boltzmann, L.	79
Britain	101
Brouwer, L.	45
Buber, M.	37

C

Cameron, Alan	66
Canada	101
Carnap, R.	37
Cassirer, E.	36
Catholics	98
Chaplin, J.	108
Cliteur, P.B.	8
Clouser, Roy	109
Cohen, H.	36
Comte, A.	36
Copi, I.M.	66

D

Dante	26
Darwin, C.	36
De Wit Duyvené, J.J.	107
Delvecchio, Giorgio	8
Democritus	20
Descartes, R.	27-28
Diemer, Harry	107
Dooyeweerd, Herman	5-9, 11-15, 17-19, 21,

	23, 25, 31, 33-34, 37, 39, 43-47, 49-50, 53-56, 58-59, 64-67, 69, 71-74, 77, 83, 93, 100-103, 107-109
Du Noüy, Lecomte	73

E

Einstein, A.	72, 74, 79-80
Empedocles	19

F

Fichte, J.	36, 74
Fichter, J.H.	51-52
France	101
Frankfurt school	37
Free University	5, 6, 13, 55
Freeman, K.	20
Foundation for Reformational Philosophy	107, 108

G

Gadamer, Hans-Georg	15
Germany	101
God	22-24, 26-28, 39, 76
Gödel, Yourgrau	48-49

Goethe, J.	36
Goudzwaard, B.	108
Grünbaum, A.	80

H

Haarlingen, Friesland	5
Habermas, J.	37, 57
Haeckel, E.	36
Hahn, H.	37
Happ, H.	21
Hartmann, N.	57
Hegel, G.	36, 63, 74
Heidegger, M.	37, 74, 77
Heisenberg, W.	72-73
Hempel, C.	37
Heraclitus	18
Herder, J.	36
Hilbert, David	45, 49-50, 74
Hobbes, T.	28
Holy Roman Empire	24
Holy Spirit	17, 22
Hommes, Henk J.	55, 108
Horkheimer, M.	37
Hume, D.	29-31
Husserl, E.	37

J

Jandl, Martin	109

Janich, P.	79
Jaspers, K.	37, 74
Jean of Jandun	100
Jesus Christ	17, 21
Journal for Historical Legal Science	56

K

Kant, Immanuel	8, 30-36, 58, 64, 66, 78
Kelsen, H.	36, 58
Kierkegaard, S.	74
Koyzis, D.T.	108
Kuyper, Abraham	7, 12
Kuyper Institute	6

L

Langemeijer, G.E.	8
Lask, E.	36
Leibniz, G.W.H.	28, 69, 78
Leiden	5
Leucippus	20
Locke, John	28-29
Lorenzen, P.	72, 73

M

Mach, E.	37
MacIver, R.M.	52
Maddy, P.	75

Maimon, S.	36
Marburgh school	36
Marx, K.	36

N

Natorp, P.	36
Netherlands	8, 101, 108
New Zealand	101
Newton, I.	30

O

Ockham	27
Ouweneel, W.J.	108

P

Parmenides	19, 20, 21
Planck, M.	72
Plato	20-21
Polak, Leo	50
Popper, Karl	15-16
Protestants	98
Pythagoreans	40

R

Rawls, J.	58
Reformation	7, 12
Renaissance	7, 64, 97
Rickert, H.	37
Roman Catholic Church	64, 97-98
Roman Empire	97, 102

Rousseau, J.	58
Russell, B.	37, 49
Ryle, G.	37

S

Sartre, J.	37
Schelling, F.	36
Schlick, M.	37
Smend, R.	57
Socrates	20
Spinoza, B.	8
Stafleu, M.D.	71, 80, 107
Stegmüller, W.	16
Strauss, D.F.M.	107, 108

T

Technical University of Delft	8
The Hague	5, 6
Troost, A.	108

U

USA, 101

V

Van Peursen, C.A.	8
Van Prinsterer, Groen	7
Vollenhoven, D. Theodor H.	7, 13
Von Padua, Marisilius	100
Von Savigny, F.	56

W

Weber, M.	37
Weideman, A.	108
Weinert, F.	73
Weyl, Hermann	45, 49
Windelband, W.	26, 37
Wittgenstein, L.	37
Wolters, Al, 23	

Z

Zeno	67, 68
Zuidema, S. U.	74

Subject Index

A

analytical philosophy	37
art	82, 90

C

Christianity	7, 98
church	12, 22, 24, 26, 64, 93, 97, 98, 101
civil private law	97, 102-104
common law	66, 103, 104
constitutional law	5, 12, 103
cosmic time	39, 77, 80, 81, 82, 83, 84, 85
Cosmonomic Idea	5, 11, 13, 108

D

divine law	23, 24

E
dualism	17, 20, 26, 36, 37

E
existentialism	37

F
faith	11, 12, 15, 16, 30, 33, 42, 46, 51, 53, 65, 83, 91, 93, 94, 102
family	94-96, 98, 101
freedom	18, 22, 26, 30, 33-37, 58, 88, 102, 103-104

G
government	5, 90, 91, 93, 99, 100, 101, 103, 104
Greek philosophy	7, 19, 21

H
historicism	14, 56, 57, 58, 68
humanism	12, 23
humanities	11, 108

I
idealism	36

J
justice	25-26, 56, 57, 58, 91

L

language	37, 42, 82, 90
linguistics	108
logic	50, 66, 69

M

mathematics	13, 27, 29, 31, 45, 49, 107
metaphysics	32, 76
Middle Ages	24, 64, 101

N

natural law	23, 24, 25-26, 54-58
natural sciences	11, 108
nature	17, 18, 19, 23-26, 27, 30, 32, 33, 34, 35-37, 42, 54, 55, 58, 62, 63, 67-69, 74, 76, 77, 79, 82, 83, 84, 95
neo-Marxism	37
neo-Platonism	23
neo-positivism	37
nominalism	27, 100

P

personalism	37
phenomenology	37
physics	30, 31, 71, 75, 78, 79, 107

political economy	90
political theory	13, 108
positivism	37, 55, 56, 57, 75, 76
postmodernism	37, 58
power	20, 22, 26, 27, 47, 53, 64, 88, 89-90, 96, 97, 100, 104
public law	103, 104

R

rationalism	15, 16
reformational philosophy	39, 107, 108
religion	11-12, 22, 64, 83
Roman Catholicism	12, 17
romanticism	36

S

salvation	22, 23
scholasticism	23
science ideal	28, 29, 30, 33, 34, 36, 37, 64
science of law	5, 13, 14, 46, 50, 53, 66, 103, 108
sociology	52, 107
space-time continuum	74, 75
state (civil government)	22, 24, 26, 27, 65, 83, 87-91, 93-94, 96, 97-104, 108

T

theology	12, 26, 27, 108
time measurement	71-72, 80

About the Author

D.F.M. Strauss served as Head of the Department of Philosophy at the University of Free State (Bloemfontein, South Africa) and Dean of the Faculty of Humanities (1998-2001). He is the General Editor of the Collected Works of the Dutch legal scholar and philosopher, Herman Dooyeweerd, and is one of five Outstanding Professors at the University of the Free State. Apart from 15 independent publications, 36 international conference papers and 20 contributions to multi-author works, he has published more than 230 articles in national and international journals, spread over 12 different scientific subject areas.

Also Available from the Author:

Being Human in God's World

More from Paideia Press:

What is Reformational Philosophy?

www.ingramcontent.com/pod-product-compliance
Lightning Source LLC
Chambersburg PA
CBHW032041290426
44110CB00012B/903